The game of golf consists of ...

"... hitting a very small ball into an even smaller hole, with weapons singularly ill-designed for the purpose."

Winston Churchill

"... playing a ball with a club from the teeing ground into the hole by a stroke or successive strokes in accordance with the Rules."

Rule 1-1.

Endorsements

"Playing by the rules is the everyday business for professional players. But getting to know the rules is also important for amateurs. First of all, they can use them to their advantage and secondly it shows respect for the spirit of the game. This book will help you gain a better understanding of the rules—which sometimes even seem confusing to the pros—and will help you to achieve better scores."

Gary Player, golf legend and Grand Slam Winner

"As a tour player I am always conscious of the fact that comprehensive knowledge of the rules, and applying them correctly, can be a decisive factor in winning or losing a game. If you previously had your work cut out getting to grips with the rules, you cannot fail to understand them if you use Yves's book. Avoid unnecessary penalty strokes and use the rules to your advantage—then you'll always be up there amongst the winners."

Alex Cejka, golf professional

"Sport is a training ground for real life. The game of golf, with its unique code of honour and its strict rules of play, is an excellent example of this—since in both sport and in everyday life playing by the rules is vital. This book explains the rules and the etiquette in a way which is easy to understand and which will add to your enjoyment of the game of golf."

Adolf Ogi, Special Advisor to the United Nations Secretary-General on Sport for Development and Peace

GOLF RULES & ETIQUETTE
CRYSTAL CLEAR

FIND THE ANSWERS TO YOUR QUESTIONS ABOUT THE RULES

by Yves Ton-That

Imprint

Publisher:
Artigo Publishing International
www.golfrulesmadeeasy.com
www.golfrules2004.com

Published 2004.

ISBN 3-909596-03-7

Acknowledgments

Books on the rules of golf cannot be written overnight. They develop and grow over a number of years—just as this one did. From its beginnings, many years ago, as a thirty-page document designed for a dozen golf students, it has today developed into a distinguished work with more than 160 pages. It is a matter of great importance to me to thank all those involved for their valuable support.

Particular thanks go to Jeff Hall and David Staebler from the United States Golf Association, as well as David Rickman from the Royal and Ancient Golf Club of St. Andrews. It was only due to their comprehensive golfing knowledge and their kind support that I was able to ensure that this book gives an accurate interpretation of the rules.

I would also like to express particular gratitude to Gary Player, Adolf Ogi and Alex Cejka—I view their support and encouragement as a great tribute, making my work even more rewarding.

Many thanks also go to all my colleagues in the media, whose kind and generous support has played a significant role in the popularity of this book.

Thanks also go to Louise for her valuable advice on the English language and help with proof reading. Many thanks to my friends Steve for the layout and cover, Roland for the excellent illustrations, Peter for creating the index and Charles for administering www.golfrulesmadeeasy.com. I would also like to thank Jacky, our model, whose kind support meant that even I looked presentable in some of the pictures.

And last but not least, to all the readers whose many suggestions, compliments and criticisms have helped the book become what it is today—thank you very much!

Author

Yves Ton-That has been a golf rules official for the past seven years and has published six books on golf, including three books on the rules, which have been published in several languages. His *Golf Rules Quick Reference Stroke Play Guide* even won second prize for being the best new product at the PGA Merchandise Show.

Ton-That has also written countless articles in his capacity as a member of the editorial team of several leading golf magazines and is internationally recognised as an expert in the field of golf rules.

Other books by the same author

- **Golf Rules Quick Reference Stroke Play Guide**
  Your handy rules guide for use on the golf course. With the Rules for the Years 2004–2007.

- **Should I Take a Drop or What ...?**
  A Collection of Hilarious Stories about the Rules of Golf.

(Information on these titles can be found at the end of the book.)

Preface

No other sport has as many rules of play and codes of conduct (etiquette) as the game of golf, and no other sport's rules are so complicated—making it very easy for players to run into trouble and unintentionally fall foul of the regulations. Consequently, mastering the rules and the etiquette is an important requirement for a successful, enjoyable game of golf.

After all, whether a player plays off scratch (with a handicap of 0) or needs far more than 100 strokes, conduct is always an important aspect of the game and even the world's best players have to comply with the rules of golf etiquette.

On the other hand, golf is unique in that it allows very good players and beginners to enjoy a round of golf together, provided that they all understand the rules, follow the code of conduct and keep up the pace of play.

Furthermore, the rules are not only made up of commands and prohibitions, they also grant numerous rights which, for example, allow the golfer to extricate himself from tricky situations without having to forfeit unnecessary strokes. Therefore whether you are able to use relief situations to your advantage or know how to avoid impending penalties, a comprehensive knowledge of the rules will most certainly be of benefit.

Moreover, one of the characteristics of the game of golf is to play against oneself (against one's own handicap) or against the course, with the player acting as his own referee. A detailed knowledge of the rules is therefore essential to honour the spirit of the game.

The following pages should help you to gain an overview of the rules of the game as well as the principles behind it. I am convinced that you can benefit from the many relief procedures which are described and that you will enjoy the game much more if you have a sound knowledge of the rules.

I hope you will enjoy reading this book and wish you continued golfing success.

Yves Ton-That

PS: The style of writing used in the text has been chosen on the basis of making the book as simple and clear as possible. In order to make this book easier to read I have dispensed with the female form (she, her etc.) to avoid the necessity for complex sentence structures. However, I am of course addressing both genders in all cases.

PPS: On my website, www.golfrulesmadeeasy.com, you can find regularly updated information on the rules of golf. If you register on this site (free of charge) I will be able to keep you up-to-date with changes to the rules and will send you information on interesting rules cases. You can also reach me by e-mail through this website—your criticisms, praise, suggestions etc. are always welcome.

Contents

Abbreviations

CR	Course Rating
exc.	except
f./ff.	following
GUR	ground under repair
Hcp	handicap
ibid.	ibidem, in the same place
in conj.	in conjunction
max.	maximum
NB	nota bene, note well
OB	out of bounds
prov.	provisional
R&A	Royal and Ancient Golf Club of St. Andrews
SR	Slope Rating
Stfd.	Stableford
USGA	United States Golf Association

Bibliography

This book is based on "The Rules of Golf" and "Decisions on the Rules of Golf" which are published by the Royal and Ancient Golf Club of St. Andrews and the United States Golf Association. The Rules of Golf are effective as of January 1, 2004, and will next be revised effective January 1, 2008.

"Golf Rules & Etiquette—Crystal Clear" is a summary of some of the rules as interpreted by the author. In case of doubt, readers should refer to the full text of the Rules and Decisions as published in the official publications.

I. Introduction

The first part of this book provides an introduction to the historical background and the systematics of the rules of golf as well as to some of the basic principles of the game and the methods of scoring. This is followed by the code of conduct for the golf course (etiquette) and subsequently by an explanation of the basic terms which are vital to an understanding of the rules.

In the practical section the most important rules will be considered and explained with the aid of illustrated examples. Certain aspects of the etiquette will also be examined once again. However the order in which the rules appear in the official rule book will not be adhered to. Instead, genuine golfing situations which often occur in the course of a round will be illustrated and used to demonstrate the relevant rules. The exact rule number concerned will be provided in the footnotes in order to enable the relevant regulation to be located easily and to be used to study the point in more depth.

The book is designed as a working text and therefore has a wide margin for your own notes. The index means it can also be used as a reference book. However it does not claim to be complete and therefore is not intended to replace the official rule book. The most important rules are explained but special cases are not considered. To keep it simple the assumption is also made that you will be playing without a team partner and without a caddie. Furthermore, the explanations of the rules are primarily related to their importance for stroke play. The variant which is less common in competitions, i.e. match play, is dealt with in an addendum.

Stroke play

In stroke play the total number of strokes is decisive. The winner is the player who required the least number of strokes to complete the round.

NB: If there are no stipulations to the contrary, the penalty for breaching a rule in stroke play is 2 PENALTY STROKES.

Match play

In match play direct opponents play against each other on a hole by hole basis. The final score is calculated by holes won and not by the total number of strokes. The winner is the player who has won the most holes (i.e. the match comes to an end as soon as a player leads by more holes than there are left to play).

NB: If there are no stipulations to the contrary, the penalty for breaching a rule in match play is LOSING THE HOLE.

II. Theory

1. History

In the early days of the game of golf, when the grass was still mowed by driving sheep across the course, there were no written rules. The majority of the players were unable to read or write anyway and therefore each course had its own "homemade" rules. When, in the spring of 1744, a small group of players who called themselves the "Gentlemen Golfers of Leith" (later "The Honourable Company of Edinburgh Golfers") asked the Magistrate of the city of Edinburgh to donate a prize for a competition which was to be held, he gave a silver club as a challenge trophy. However the city fathers attached a condition to the prize, namely that it was to be an open competition with as many participants as possible. And this of course necessitated that universally applicable guidelines were drawn up and recorded in writing. Thus, the first 13 golf rules came into existence.

When, in the year 1754, an open competition was also to be held at the golf club in St. Andrews (at that time neither royal nor ancient), those responsible at the club adopted the aforementioned 13 laws unchanged. As the years went on, the Edinburgh golfers faced financial problems, moved to a different course and at times even had to cease operation entirely, making it impossible for them to continue developing the rules of golf. Therefore all eyes suddenly turned to St. Andrews and most clubs adopted its rules unaltered. This did, however, cause one or two problems as the R&A constantly developed their rules, sometimes also referring to purely local circumstances and provided rulings for situations which did not apply to other courses. This should come as no surprise as the R&A had issued their rules for their course alone—they were not particularly interested in whether or not these rules were adopted by other golf clubs. Even in 1885, when vociferous demands were made for the R&A to standardise its rules and issue them as the highest authority for all golf clubs, they still saw no reason to take action. The rules committee was only established five years later and the R&A thereby gained, almost reluctantly, a leading position on rules issues which it still enjoys today.

At almost the same time, namely in 1894, the "United States Golf Association" (USGA) became established as the leading organisation responsible for golf in America and Mexico. They too adopted the R&A rules, but supplemented them with a great many of their own, subsequently resulting in numerous discrepancies arising between the regulations in Europe and those in America.

It was only in 1951 that Britain and America decided to work together on issues relating to the rules and they consequently produced a revised edition, valid from 1952. But those who thought that a uniform system had been developed once and for all were sadly mistaken. Only the rules were standardised—Local Rules, appendices and Decisions were still left to the sole discretion of each individual association. For a number of years this led to the situation whereby those playing under the R&A rules used a smaller ball than the Americans and that further discrepancies arose in a number of other respects. With an extensive revision in 1984, the rules were finally brought in line with each other, ensuring that today, the entire golfing world plays in accordance with the same rules.

Since then the rules have been revised every four years by a commission of experts, made up of members of the R&A and the USGA. The last review took place with effect from January 1st 2004.

2. Systematics

The rule book is formulated in English by the R&A and the USGA and it is then translated into the relevant languages by the national golf associations. However in the event of doubt, the original English version is the definitive version for interpreting the rules.

The official version of the rules of golf is divided into three sections:

Section I—Etiquette
The first section in the rule book contains the regulations on conduct on the golf course (etiquette). The high degree of importance placed on etiquette is underlined by the fact that this section appears at the beginning of the book.

Section II—Definitions
51 terms are defined and explained. In order to be able to understand the rules which follow it is imperative that these definitions have been clearly understood and internalised.

Section III—The Rules of Play
This section contains the actual rules of play. There are only 34 of these rules however they take up the greatest part of the 140 pages of the rule book.

The rule book is supplemented by three appendices. These contain special provisos and recommendations on Local Rules and conditions of competition, which are mainly of relevance to Committees. In addition to this the appendices also contain detailed guidelines on the design and construction of clubs and balls. These however are mainly aimed at the relevant manufacturers.

The *Decisions* have a similar level of importance as the rules—these are decisions on precedents which are not clearly dealt with by the rules. They are published as a compendium every two years and are mainly of relevance to referees.

In addition to the rule book there are other regulations which are to be observed. These include the *Local Rules* in particular, which are drawn up individually for each course. They take the course's individual characteristics into account, while still being in agreement with the basic stipulations of the rules of golf. In some cases they are only valid for a limited period of time. The Local Rules can be read on the notice board or on the back of the score card. Finally, *instructions* from the golf course staff (e.g. the captain, marshals, rangers, starters and greenkeepers) are also important—they are to be followed at all times.

The particular significance of etiquette and its importance in preventing accidents determines that its guidelines are to be obeyed consistently by everyone, at all times. Whether you are playing a friendly game or in a competition, whether you are alone, with friends or with strangers, etiquette must always be adhered to without exception.

Instructions from the course staff are also to be obeyed at all times, as these usually involve matters of extreme importance or the protection of certain areas of the golf course.

There is a little more room for manoeuvre with the rules of golf themselves. In competitions the rules must be strictly adhered to and, in cases of doubt, the rule book or possibly a referee must be consulted. On the other hand in private, friendly games you can deal with the rules in a somewhat more flexible way and, for example, give short putts. However you should ensure that no one else is disturbed by your relaxed attitude to the rules.

An unwritten "golden" rule of golf says "During a friendly round be guided by your sense of sportsmanship and play the course as you find it and the ball as it lies, if a rule does not explicitly permit anything different. However in official competitions consult the rule book in cases of doubt. Never try to gain an undue, unfair advantage."

However this advice should not be followed to the letter. It certainly is advisable to apply the rules consistently in private rounds as well and, if time permits, to consult the rule book or allow discussions on rules issues to take place. This will help you to become acquainted with the rules and to develop a certain routine, thus ensuring that in a competition you are not suddenly confronted with a completely new situation which you have always ignored in friendly games. (If, for example, you get into the habit of giving short putts (mentioned above) during friendly rounds you could make the mistake of picking up a ball perched on the lip of the hole in a competition. As this is not allowed the ball has to be put back under penalty of 1 stroke and then has to be holed. If you do not do this immediately you will be disqualified.)

The section on etiquette and the section on the rules both contain commands and prohibitions. The fundamental difference is that penalty strokes are not usually imposed as the sanction for breaches of etiquette but cautions are given instead (the player is reprimanded). However serious breaches are punished with disqualification, expulsion from the course or a temporary or even permanent suspension.

On the other hand breaches of the rules are punished with penalty strokes (usually 1 or 2 penalty strokes, which can accumulate). In serious cases which cannot be remedied the penalty of disqualification is a definite possibility.

If a player deliberately breaches a rule of play in order to gain an advantage (cheating), the player will be banned from playing as an extra penalty, as this also involves a breach of etiquette.

Sanctions. In golf, different sanctions are imposed depending on the type and severity of the breach.

	Breach of etiquette	Breach of the rules
Unintentional, minor breach	Reprimand, caution	1 penalty stroke (playing error)
Careless, avoidable breach	Warning, competition ban	2 penalty strokes (breach of the rules)
Inexcusable, irreparable breach	A ban from playing, expulsion, disqualification	Disqualification

3. The golf course complex

The golf course complex usually comprises the clubhouse, a practice area (driving range) and the playing area—the actual course.

3.1. The clubhouse

Most golf courses have an extensive infrastructure based in the clubhouse—the secretary's office, the pro shop, changing rooms, restaurant etc.

3.2. The driving range

The driving range mainly consists of a large grassed area bordered by numerous teeing grounds. Several players practice along side each other by playing shots onto the grass. The aim of the driving range is to give players the opportunity to practice those shots which are played most often during a round, therefore the training ground is usually supplemented with a bunker to practice bunker shots, a chipping and pitching green for approach shots and a putting green to practice holing-out.

3.3. The golf course

The golf course is divided into 18 holes. Some golf courses only have 9 holes which each have to be played twice during a complete round of golf. A differentiation is made between the first 9 holes (front nine) and the second nine (back nine); these are also described as "Out" and "In" on the score card.
The individual holes are also divided into different areas:

- Teeing ground
  The teeing ground is made up of a level, closely-mown area, which is usually raised. It forms the starting point of each hole to be played. In order to do justice to different golfing abilities each hole has several teeing grounds which are marked with different colours.

The golf course complex

- **Fairway**

  The closely-mown area between the teeing ground and the green is called the fairway. This is the area where the ball should land and be played from.

- **Semi-rough**

  The semi-rough (also called the first or second cut) is the area which borders the edge of the fairway. The grass is somewhat longer than on the fairway and the area is an interim stage between the fairway and the rough. If a ball rolls off the fairway it usually comes to a stop in the semi-rough which prevents it from getting lost.

- **Rough**

  The rough is the name given to long or uncut grass, bushes and wooded areas on the golf course.

- **Hazards**

  —Water hazard

  Water hazards are natural or artificially created water courses (rivers, ponds, lakes, the sea etc.). They are usually marked by coloured stakes (yellow = regular water hazard, red = lateral water hazard).

  —Bunker

  Bunkers are sunken areas from which the earth has been removed and replaced with sand.

- **Fringe**

  The fringe has similar characteristics to the green except that the grass is not cut quite so short. It forms an intermediate stage between the fairway and the green. As far as the rules are concerned the fringe is *not* a part of the green.

- **Green**

  The green is the name given to the low-cut area of grass around the hole which undergoes special preparation. This area is where putts are taken.

- Out of bounds

  Out of bounds refers to the area which, according to the rules, is not a part of the course. A player is not allowed to play a ball which is out of bounds. These are often areas which should not be walked on or at least which should not be played on. Out of bounds is usually marked in white (posts, fences, walls etc.), however sometimes it is not marked with a colour and is only specified in the Local Rules (e.g. if a road defines the margin of the out of bounds area).

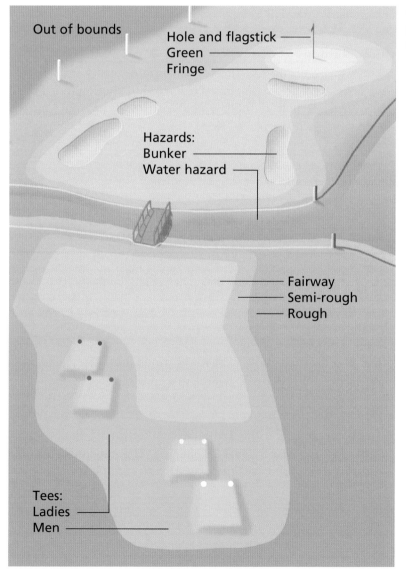

Out of bounds

Hole and flagstick
Green
Fringe

Hazards:
Bunker
Water hazard

Fairway
Semi-rough
Rough

Tees:
Ladies
Men

Areas of a hole. The entire golf course as well as every hole is divided into different areas.

4. Score card

The score card documents the number of strokes played in a round. It is divided into the following sections:

- **Player**
  The player's first name and surname.

- **Hcp**
  The player's Handicap Index/ Course Handicap.

- **Competition**
  The name and form of the competition (possibly information on which tees are to be played from and, if the round is not to be started at hole number 1, information is provided on the hole which will be played first).

- **Date**
  Date of the competition.

- **Marker (also called scorer)**
  Column for entering the number of strokes taken by the marker (he can enter his own score in this column as a cross-reference).

- **Hole**
  The number of the hole.

- **Men/ Ladies**
  The length of the hole from the various tees. The distance to the middle of the green is measured in each case.

- **Hcp**
  The hole's level of difficulty (is needed to allocate the handicap strokes in accordance with Stableford). The most difficult hole is given the value 1 and the easiest is given number 18.

- **Par**
  The par is the expected number of strokes for the hole.

Player							Hcp			
Jeff Miller							19.8/24			

Competition	Audi Quattro Final						Date			
	Stroke play/ back tees						07.08.04			

Marker	Hole	Men champion	Men medal	Ladies champion	Ladies medal	Hcp	Par	Player			+ 0 -
6	1	380	345	335	315	7	4	5			
4	2	370	350	315	295	9	4	5			
5	3	490	475	445	420	15	5	5			
4	4	175	160	155	140	11	3	5			
5	5	325	275	270	235	17	4	5			
6	6	560	520	495	460	3	5	6			
5	7	195	170	165	145	13	3	4			
6	8	400	385	355	340	1	4	7			
6	9	410	365	360	320	5	4	8̶ 10 *Clar h.*			
47	Out	3305	3045	2895	2670		36	52			
5	10	300	275	265	255	18	4	4			
5	11	360	320	305	280	10	4	5			
5	12	480	470	445	415	12	5	5			
4	13	370	345	330	290	2	4	3			
5	14	150	140	130	125	16	3	4			
6	15	355	325	315	285	4	4	6			
4	16	370	340	325	295	6	4	4			
5	17	210	180	175	150	8	3	5			
5	18	460	450	405	390	14	5	6			
44	In	3055	2845	2695	2485		36	42			
47	Out	3305	3045	2895	2670		36	52			
91	Total	6360	5890	5590	5155		72	94			

Course/ Slope Rating				Hcp	24			
☐ 73/130	☐ 75/132			Net	70			
☐ 71/128	☐ 73/124							

Player	Marker
J. Muller	*Clar hm*

- **Player**
  Column for entering the number of strokes taken by the player.

- **+ 0 –**
  Column for entering the results for (rarely played) Par competitions.

- **Course/ Slope Rating**
  Indices which indicate the level of difficulty of a course and which are used to calculate the handicap (see page 26ff.).

- **Net**
  Net result—total number of strokes after deducting the handicap.

- **Player/ Marker (also called scorer)**
  Areas for the player and the marker to confirm the result by means of their signatures.
  NB: Erroneous or unclear entries on the score card are not simply to be written over with bold writing. It is better to cross them out and record the correct entries along side (as illustrated). It is then advisable for the marker to sign the new entries as well.

- **Local Rules**
  The individual Local Rules are printed on the back of the score card.

5. Par and the Slope System

The par refers to the number of strokes expected to be played for a hole or a round. A par 3 hole should therefore be played taking 3 strokes and 72 strokes should be used to play a par 72 course. There are par 3, par 4 and par 5 holes. The main factor involved in determining the par is the length of the hole. This is based on the assumption that 2 putts will be needed on the green to hole the ball. In accordance with this principle the green should be reached with one stroke on a par 3 and then 2 further strokes should be needed to hole-out. Correspondingly, 2 strokes are calculated for reaching the green on a par 4 and 3 strokes on a par 5. The total of the individual pars provides the par for the whole course. Most golf courses have an overall par of 72 (4 x par 3, 10 x par 4, 4 x par 5), however there are also par 70 and par 71 courses for example.

If a player completes a hole using the intended number of strokes this is called playing to par. If he needs one stroke more than intended it is called a bogey; two strokes over par is a double bogey. If he needs one stroke less than intended it is called a birdie; two strokes under par is called an eagle and three strokes under par is an albatross (also known as a double-eagle). If a player holes-out using only one stroke it is called a hole-in-one. This usually only happens on a par 3.

	2 strokes (3 under par)	=	albatross
	3 strokes (2 under par)	=	eagle
	4 strokes (1 under par)	=	birdie
Example: par 5	5 strokes	=	par
	6 strokes (1 over par)	=	bogey
	7 strokes (2 over par)	=	double-bogey
	8 strokes (3 over par)	=	triple-bogey

Terminology. In golf, every score has a name. All above-average scores are characterised by the name of a bird.

Par and the Slope System

The term Slope System refers to a method of rating golf courses which allows the different levels of difficulty of the individual courses to be taken into consideration.

Using a complex procedure, the course is measured and rated and its level of difficulty is determined for each category of teeing ground (white, yellow, blue etc.). The total length of the holes and numerous other characteristics, such as the closeness of out of bounds margins, the arrangement and number of hazards, topography etc., are taken into account. The level of difficulty is indicated by the ratings. The system is based on two values in each case.

- **Course Rating (CR)**
  This rating modifies the course's par and is the same as the par or only slightly different from it. It is the result which a scratch golfer should achieve. It is therefore possible that a particularly long and demanding par 72 course has a CR of 74.

- **Slope Rating (SR)**
  This rating indicates the degree to which a player's handicap must be modified in order to master the different levels of difficulty on the course. It is a minimum of 55 and a maximum of 155. The higher the SR, the more demanding the course is. A course with an average level of difficulty has an SR of 113.

6. Handicap

The handicap is a number which represents a golfer's playing ability. To put it simply, it is the number of strokes which a player should be over par after 18 holes, i.e. the number of strokes which he should need in excess of the course par.

Whereas golf is played to the same rules the world over, there are a wide variety of vastly differing handicap regulations in different countries. The USGA handicap is by nature very optimistic and tends to represent a player's *potential* scoring ability, i.e. he will usually need more strokes than his handicap would suggest. The reasoning behind this system is to attempt to stop a player taking part in a competition with a handicap which is too high, thus giving him an advantage over the rest of the field (players who do this are often referred to as sandbaggers). In contrast to this, the method of calculation is much more realistic in other countries and the handicap corresponds to the score which the player is most likely to achieve. This is to prevent players trying to reduce their handicap for appearances' sake (so-called vanity handicaps).

6.1. Getting and adjusting a handicap

As the regulations differ so greatly from country to country and are based on extremely complicated methods of calculation, we will limit ourselves to an explanation of a few basic principles. There is no need to rack your brains to work out your handicap—let your club calculate it for you as they have the relevant computer programmes to do it.

The first and highest handicap is usually 36, and once you have got this handicap you can gradually improve on it by playing under it.

In order to be able to do justice to the various levels of difficulty on the different courses, the handicap is usually adjusted for each course and even for each set of tees (back or front tees, men's or ladies' tees)—the handicap is increased for difficult courses and it is reduced correspondingly on easier courses. The handicap is therefore divided into an index and a practical value derived from this theoretical value. This is called the Playing Handicap or the Course Handicap*:

- **Handicap Index (also called Exact Handicap)**
  A reference value calculated exactly to one decimal point.

- **Course Handicap (also called Playing Handicap)**
  Adapted handicap, i.e. strokes allocated taking the level of difficulty of the course into account.

When "handicap" is mentioned in general, the official Handicap Index is meant. This (neutral) handicap is calculated for a theoretical, totally average course, with a Slope of 113 and which has the same value for both the par and the Course Rating.
The Course Handicap corresponds to the Handicap Index but it is adapted to the level of difficulty of the course about to be played. It is calculated by means of a complicated formula and is then rounded up or down.

$$\text{Course Hcp} = \text{Hcp Index} \times (\text{SR}/113) + (\text{CR} - \text{Par})$$

As a player you only have to know your Hcp Index. In the event of a competition, the relevant Course Handicap will be calculated for you by the Committee or you can simply read it off a table which is pinned up in every golf club.
To summarise, a player has a different Course Hcp for each course, depending on which set of tees he is playing from, however he only has one Hcp Index.
If a player plays over or under his (Course) Hcp, the Hcp Index is increased or reduced. As calculating the Hcp adjustments is extremely complicated, Hcp administration is carried out by the player's home club. However the responsibility for this nevertheless lies with the player, i.e. he has to keep informed of his own Hcp and submit all his scores, even those from competitions played at other clubs.

*This does not apply in the UK under the so-called CONGU system. In accordance with this system a player only has one handicap which is not adjusted for each course.

The handicap system is another feature of golf which makes the sport unique and which sets it apart from other sports. It allows golfers of different ability levels to play against each other with an equal chance on any course. In other words, even the novice can play against a top golfer, and grandchildren can compete on fair terms with their grandfather.

6.2. Excursus: Amateurs and pros

If a player decides to become involved with the game of golf on a professional basis he has to change from being an amateur to a professional. Pros are professional competition players (touring professionals) and golf instructors (teaching professionals)—none of whom have a handicap.

There has been a strict differentiation between amateurs and professionals since the very beginnings of the sport. Amateurs are expected to play golf for golf's sake and are not permitted to accept remuneration for their golfing success. This is to ensure that the pleasure of playing golf is at the forefront for amateurs and that neither the game of golf nor individual players are corrupted by money or monetary benefits. Therefore only professionals are, for example, allowed to receive money for giving lessons, sign sponsorship deals, play for monetary prizes or accept prizes which exceed a value of US$ 750.00 (£500.00/ 750.00 Euros).

7. Stableford

The term Stableford (Stfd.) refers to a form of scoring by which the number of points scored in accordance with the Stableford system is decisive and not the total number of strokes taken. The player is awarded the following number of points at each hole depending on his result:

Stableford points. In a Stableford competition, the total number of strokes is not important, players are awarded points based on their score for a hole.

Albatross (3 under par)	= 5 points
Eagle (2 under par)	= 4 points
Birdie (1 under par)	= 3 points
Par	= 2 points
Bogey (1 over par)	= 1 point
Double-bogey and worse (2 or more over par or no result at all)	= 0 points

The advantage of this game is that extremely poor results on certain holes do not have such a significant effect. While in stroke play a very "poor hole" can ruin the overall score, in Stableford it merely means that no points are awarded. As soon as a player has played so many strokes on one hole that he can no longer score any points he is obliged to pick up the ball. This speeds up the pace of play considerably and therefore competitions played under the Stableford system are very popular for beginners. The rules which apply to stroke play are valid for Stableford competitions.

A distinction is made between the gross number of strokes taken and the net score. The winner is the player who has scored the highest number of points.

7.1. Gross score

For the gross score the points are allocated to the various holes in accordance with the actual number of strokes taken, based on the above table.

7.2. Net score

For the net score, points are allocated after deduction of the handicap strokes. In order to do this the handicap is first allocated to the individual holes and the player is given so-called handicap strokes. The level of difficulty of the individual holes is taken into account in this process (handicap column on the scorecard; the most difficult hole is given a handicap of 1 and the easiest is handicap 18).

> Example:
> A player with a handicap of 36 is given 2 handicap strokes at each hole.
> A player with a handicap of 30 is given 1 handicap stroke at each hole, plus an additional stroke on the 12 most difficult holes.
> A player with a handicap of 6 is therefore only given 1 handicap stroke at each of the 6 most difficult holes.

The handicap strokes are then deducted from the actual number of strokes at each hole and the Stfd. points are calculated on the basis of this net result.

> Example:
> A player records a bogey on one hole. He is given 1 gross point for this. However if he has been given a handicap stroke at this hole it is deducted and the net result corresponds to a par for which he is then given 2 net points.

If a player scores 36 net points he has played to his handicap in accordance with Stfd. If he scores more than 36 points each point above this number means that he has played under his handicap by the corresponding number of strokes (or if he scores less than 36 points he has played over his handicap by the corresponding number of strokes).

The allocation of handicap strokes and the calculation of the Stableford points is the responsibility of the Competition Committee.

Stableford

The player therefore only has to record his actual number of strokes or, if he has picked up his ball, he records a no-score.

> Example:
> A player with a handicap of 24 is given 24 handicap strokes—one stroke for each hole and an additional stroke at the 6 most difficult holes. If he then scores 40 Stableford points he has played under his handicap by four stroke in accordance with Stableford—therefore his score is equivalent to a handicap of 20.

Marker	Hole	Men champion	Men medal	Ladies champion	Ladies medal	Hcp	Par	Player	Stableford gross	net
6	1	380	345	335	315	7	4	5	1	2
4	2	370	350	315	295	9	4	5	1	2
5	3	490	475	445	420	15	5	5	2	3
4	4	175	160	155	140	11	3	5	-	1
5	5	325	275	270	235	17	4	5	1	2
6	6	560	520	495	460	3	5	6	1	3
5	7	195	170	165	145	13	3	4	1	2
6	8	400	385	355	340	1	4	7	-	1
6	9	410	365	360	320	5	4	-	-	-
	Out	3305	3045	2895	2670		36		7	16
5	10	300	275	265	255	18	4	4	2	3
5	11	360	320	305	280	10	4	5	1	2
5	12	480	470	445	415	12	5	5	2	3
4	13	370	345	330	290	2	4	3	3	5
5	14	150	140	130	125	16	3	4	1	2
6	15	355	325	315	285	4	4	6	-	2
4	16	370	340	325	295	6	4	4	2	4
5	17	210	180	175	150	8	3	5	-	1
5	18	460	450	405	390	14	5	6	1	2
	In	3055	2845	2695	2485		36		12	24
	Out	3305	3045	2895	2670		36		7	16
	Total	6360	5890	5590	5155		72		19	40

Player
Jeff Miller

Competition
Audi Quattro Cup
Stableford/ back tees

Hcp
19.8/24

Date
07.17.04

Course/ Slope Rating

☐ 73/130 ▨ 75/132
▨ 71/128 ▨ 73/124

Hcp

Net

Player
J. Miller

Marker

Stableford. *The Stableford form of scoring has the decided advantage that extremely bad holes do not have such a significant effect. Also, not every hole has to be completed—a player can pick up his ball and give up the hole. This speeds up the pace of play considerably.*

8. Etiquette

In the early days, the etiquette was just a series of unwritten rules as it involved nothing more than common sense and good manners, applied to the specific circumstances surrounding the game of golf. However, as golf underwent extensive development it was discovered that the etiquette was not being passed on adequately, so today it forms a fixed—albeit very brief—part of the rule book ("Section I—Etiquette; behaviour on the course").

The extreme importance of etiquette can be seen in the fact that it is placed first in the official edition of the rules of golf, before the actual rules themselves. However, the etiquette is not a part of the rules in the strict sense, as, first and foremost, it provides a standard for the players' interaction with each other and their treatment of the course, rather than for the game itself. Furthermore, breaches of etiquette are not penalised with penalty strokes. Instead, disciplinary measures, such as warnings, a ban from the course or a playing ban are usually imposed by the Committee.

Despite the sanctions available, the powers that be at the USGA and the R&A were under the impression that too little attention was still being paid to the etiquette, and therefore the penalty of disqualification has been introduced for particularly serious breaches as from the year 2004 onwards. This is an alarming development inasmuch as complying with the etiquette should be a matter of course for every true golfer and it therefore should not actually be necessary to impose this type of punishment.

The aim of etiquette is to ensure safety, optimum pace of play and fairness. In addition to this the etiquette also contains important regulations on caring for and maintaining the course and finally it also deals with golfing traditions.

The etiquette is absolutely indispensable in ensuring that the game of golf can be enjoyed. It applies to everyone, at all times—as no etiquette means no golf! Summed up into one sentence it means nothing more than:

Always conduct yourself in the way that you would like others to conduct themselves.

8.1. Safety measures

Prevention of accidents. Golf can be dangerous, therefore always ensure that no one will be put at risk due to a swing or stroke which you are about to make.

Ensure that the area of swing is free. Before making a swing always ensure that no one is standing so close to you that they could be hit by your club.

Ensure that the direction of swing is free. Never swing towards an area where people are standing—stones, sand and other objects could be moved unintentionally and cause injury. Even if you are taking a practice swing without making contact with the ground you must also bear in mind that in rare, but extremely dangerous cases the club head can become detached from the shaft (e.g. due to the connecting piece rusting through).

Ensure that the target area is free. Never play before the players in front of you are out of range. You must always judge this based on your best possible shot, adding on extra distance as a precautionary measure. Also, do not play too close behind the players in front of you even if they are out of range. On par 3 holes you should only ever tee-off when the group in front has left the green.
Show particular consideration if golf course staff, especially greenkeepers, are in the target area or in the near vicinity. These people carry out important work on the golf course and in doing so are permanently exposed to danger from balls in flight (this danger is often increased as greenkeepers cannot hear shouts of warning when, for example, they are mowing the grass). Therefore never play until the person in question has seen you and can follow the flight of your ball.

Avoid ricochets. Avoid trying to hit a ball closely around a tree, wall or other similar object which is directly ahead of you. The ball could rebound from it, seriously injuring your fellow-competitors or yourself.

Etiquette

Area of swing. *Check that no one is standing within your swing radius and do not swing in the direction of other people in the near vicinity.*

Target area. *Check that no one is standing in your target area and never play a shot before the players in front of you are out of range.*

Rebounds. *Never try to play close past an object. If the ball was to rebound you would probably not have enough time to get out of the way.*

8.2. Shout of warning

Fore. If someone could be endangered by your ball, even if the probability of being hit is only slight, then call fore immediately, several times and as loudly as possible (fore is an internationally-recognised warning in golf).

Errant shots. Call fore if a ball is heading towards people or if you lose sight of a ball which was heading in a direction where people could be standing (e.g. the ball has flown over a group of trees or a barn and you do not know whether there is another fairway or green behind it).
Always remember that golf balls in flight reach top speeds of up to 150 mph and consequently they can turn into deadly projectiles. Therefore do not hesitate—it is better to shout too often than to take the slightest risk.

Shout loudly. Shout loudly enough for a golfer 200 yards away to hear your warning. Fellow-competitors should also call—not only the player himself.

Fore is the traditional and globally accepted shout of warning in golf. However non-golfers, such as walkers or hikers, often do not react to fore, therefore it is then better to call "Careful" or "Watch out".

Apology. Even if no one was hit, an apology is still expected as a matter of courtesy.

8.3. How to respond to a warning shout

Defensive reaction. If you hear someone shout fore duck down immediately and protect your head with your arms.

Always react and react quickly. Always protect yourself when you hear fore, even if it is quiet and sounds a long way off—calls are very difficult to hear against the wind or over a long distance. React quickly, without first looking round to see where the danger is coming from.

Defensive reaction. Duck down and protect yourself as soon as you hear someone calling fore. If possible, take cover behind your golf trolley, cart, a tree or another suitable object.

8.4. Pace of play

Speed. Always play and walk quickly and avoid unnecessary loss of time.

Max. search time. During practice rounds you should not take up all of the 5 minutes' search time, especially if there is little hope of finding the ball from the outset. Please also bear in mind that it makes no sense at all to spend time searching for a ball out of bounds as it could no longer be played anyway.

Readiness. It is always the turn of the player whose ball is the farthest away from the hole. Ensure that you are always aware of when it is your turn to play and that you prepare for the stroke in advance.

Practice swings. Bear in mind that too many practice swings delay the game and could annoy fellow-competitors. Furthermore, each practice swing does not only take up time but also uses up strength.

Freeing up the green. Clear the green immediately after finishing a hole and only record your scores at the next tee or on the way to it. Congratulations, commiserations, discussions and reviews of the hole must wait until the flag has been put back and you have left the green.

Placing equipment strategically. Always leave your golf bag, trolley or cart level with where you are and, if you have reached the green, in the direction of the next tee.

Provisional ball. To avoid having to walk back unnecessarily you should always play a provisional ball if you are in doubt as to whether you will find your ball or not. It is therefore advisable always to have a spare ball to hand.

Approximate times. The following approximate times for playing 18 holes are to be used as a rough guide. Of course, the particular situation involved is to be taken into consideration in each case (competition/ friendly game, hilly/ level course, on foot/ with a cart, extremely high temperatures/ pleasant temperatures etc.).

2-ball match: 3 hours and 45 minutes

3-ball match: 4 hours

4-ball match: 4 hours and 15 minutes

Suggested times. Please try to keep to these suggested times if at all possible. A golfing saying states "only a fast game is a good game".

8.5. Priority

Faster groups. In order to ensure that the game can be played at an acceptable pace and that queues are avoided, slower players are to let following players pass. The following group is to be invited to play through by means of a clear signal.
NB: Slow play and queues are the most common cause of debate on the golf course. Therefore, please let the following group through *immediately* if the situation makes this necessary. In particular, do not wait until the following players request this or until they even make a complaint. Letting a group through is not a humiliation—on the contrary it shows generosity and sportsmanship.

Max. 4-ball match. A maximum of four players are usually allowed to play in a group.

2-ball, 3-ball and 4-ball matches. Faster groups always have priority over slower ones. In practice, this often means that 2-ball matches have priority over 3-ball and 4-ball matches. However, please note that this regulation is reversed on many courses at the weekend so that 4-ball matches always have priority over 3-ball matches, who have priority over 2-ball matches, irrespective of their speed. The aim of this ruling is to use the course to its full capacity and to give as many players as possible the opportunity to play golf. This ruling is usually recorded on the score card or on the notice board.

Individual players. Individual players do not have any rights on the course and must allow all following players to pass. In fact it could be said that they are at the mercy of everyone else. However in practice this ruling is often not adhered to particularly strictly. The quicker individual players are often let through, especially if the course is not too busy.

Losing touch or long searches. Following players are to be let through by any group who cannot keep up with the normal pace of the game, who lose touch with the group in front and who have more than one free hole in front of them. This is also the case if a ball is not found straight away and it is clear from the very beginning that the search could take a long time. Please remember to immediately invite the following group to pass through and not only after the allowed 5 minutes search time has already expired.

Shortened rounds. Any group which is playing a complete round always has priority over those groups playing a shortened round or who are playing the holes in a different order to that stipulated. In particular you should be careful not to cut off the players coming from the ninth hole if you start your round at the tenth tee. (Please bear in mind that restrictions are often applied to starting from the tenth tee and sometimes express permission is even required.)

A *B*

__Letting through.__ If circum-stances require, invite follow-ing players to pass through with a clear waving signal. If, however, you yourself are invited to play through, indi-cate your intentions clearly— should you wish to pass through hold your club up in the air (A). If you do not want to pass through indicate this by refusing with a clear waving signal (B).

Letting through correctly. When letting other players through you should move to a safe place at the side of the fairway, taking your equipment with you. You should only start playing again when the players who have been let through are out of range.

8.6. Care and maintenance

Consideration. Please care for and maintain the course whenever possible. The best basic principle to follow is to always leave the course in a better condition than you found it in. Incidentally, this does not just apply to your home course but should also be taken as read on other courses too.

Teeing ground. Never position golf bags and trolleys on the teeing ground—they should always be placed next to it. Practice swings are also to be made to the side rather than on the teeing ground itself. Pieces of grass which are hit out (divots) are not to be replaced on the teeing ground—the holes are to be filled in with the sand and grass seed mixture provided.

Divots. Avoid damaging the grass when making practice swings round the course. Always replace divots and tread them in well. Please also make the effort to replace divots which other players have forgotten.
NB: In some parts of the world, depending on the type of grass, *replacing* divots is not always the best remedy; in this case the divot holes should be filled in with a mixture of sand and seed (which is usually provided in a box at the rear of the cart or on the tee).

Positioning equipment. Golf bags and trolleys are always to be left outside hazards. Furthermore, the rough is also to be avoided as far as possible.
If you are using a golf cart please stay on the paths provided whenever possible. Golf carts can damage the grass and therefore in many cases they are not permitted on the fairways at all. Please observe the related safety stipulations and traffic regulations at all times.

Bunkers. Always enter the bunker from the shallow side even if this is not the shortest way to the ball. Carefully smooth out your marks with the rake after you have finished playing from the bunker (if there is not a rake available you can also level out your marks with a club).

Fairplay. *Raking the bunker is only one of many responsibilities which a golfer must fulfil. He is also responsible for repairing divots, pitch marks and spike marks as well as for leaving the course in top condition. The idea behind this is to ensure that following players are provided with the same, fair conditions that you would like to have for yourself.*

Green and fringe. The green and the fringe require utmost care and attention. You are not permitted to position your golf bag on this area nor to pull your trolley across it. Especial care must also be given to the area in the near vicinity of the green, in particular the area between bunkers and the edge of the green.

Repair pitch marks with a pitch repairer or, if you do not have one to hand, with a tee. Also please avoid damaging the course with your spikes (do not drag your feet when walking). Carefully repair spike marks on the green *after* completing the hole. Do not step too close to the hole and avoid fraying the edges of the hole by removing or replacing the flagstick without due care. Lay the flagstick down carefully, off the green whenever possible. Please avoid leaning on your putter when removing the ball from the hole.

Tidiness. Please dispose of broken tees in the container provided and do not leave any other litter on the course. Please also make an effort to pick up any rubbish that players ahead of you have left behind.

Cigarette ends on the course are a cause of particular annoyance. Therefore ashtrays which can be attached to a golf bag or a cart have been developed for golfers who smoke.

8.7. Fairness, courtesy and politeness

Good behaviour. Please conduct yourself in a quiet, fair manner on the course and avoid any sort of conduct which could disturb other players.

The honour. Always ensure that the correct order of play is adhered to (in particular please make sure that you observe the ruling concerning who has the honour to tee-off first). If you inadvertently tee-up your ball too soon you should remove both the ball and the tee until it is your turn.

Comments. Do not comment on every stroke and in particular do not complain about how badly your game is going at the moment and that you actually can play much better.
Also, show restraint as far as shots made by your fellow-competitors are concerned and only praise them for really good strokes. Weaker players should ensure that they do not praise good golfers for shots which they themselves are totally unsatisfied with. Furthermore, a stroke is not a success just because it looks good in the air but only if it lands in the right place. Therefore wait until the ball has stopped before giving any praise.
Tips are often well-intentioned but should only be given if the player has asked for help. Please bear in mind that if you are playing in a competition only the caddie or the team partner are permitted to give a player advice (a breach of this rule would result in 2 penalty strokes).

Wrong fairway. If you accidentally hit your ball onto a neighbouring fairway you can usually continue playing as normal from there. However please ensure that you do not impede the group playing the hole in question. You do not have priority on the wrong fairway!

Quietness and positioning. While a player is preparing for a shot, or would like to play one, it is best to stand opposite him. Do not stand too close to him or behind him, nor on the extension of his line of play. Avoid making any noise or movement at this time. Also, please ensure that your shadow does not fall within his line of sight.

If you feel that something is disturbing your game do not hesitate to point it out (e.g. ask your fellow-player to move back a bit or to stand still). It makes no sense at all to only make your comments after the stroke has been played and even to blame your fellow-competitor for the fluffed shot.

Position. In general you should always be level with the ball to be played. Walking ahead is distracting and could also be dangerous.

Consideration. Always bear in mind that there are other groups on the course who could be disturbed by your conduct. You should therefore also stand quietly when players from other groups are preparing to play a stroke in the near vicinity. You should show particular consideration when passing other greens or tees.

Greetings. It is customary to greet other players on the golf course—including those you do not know.

Greetings on the golf course.
A silent greeting, including to players you do not know, is accepted behaviour on the golf course.

Other balls. Please leave other balls where they are (unless no other players can be seen far and wide and you are absolutely sure that the ball you have found is no longer in play).

Looking for a ball. Please help your fellow-competitors to look for the ball. This saves time and you will also be glad of their help.

Line of putt. The line of putt is sacrosanct. Never walk on your own line of putt nor on that of a fellow-competitor.

Tending the flag. Tend the flag for your fellow-competitors.

Self-control. Refrain from any outbursts of emotion on the golf course.

No temper tantrums. Swearing or ramming clubs into the ground, throwing them or breaking them in half etc. is absolutely out of the question on the golf course and would be punished severely.

Participate and complete the round. If you have registered for a competition you must take part (in the event of illness please inform the organiser). You are also obliged to play the round to the end even if you do not feel like it or are in poor form. A game may only be interrupted or suspended in exceptional circumstances e.g. in the event of illness, accident, darkness, storms with a risk of lightning (whereas torrential rain alone is not a reason to discontinue a competition round).

Excursus: Storm with lightning is life-threatening, especially on the golf course. Therefore find shelter *in good time*—when there is less than 30 seconds between the lightning and the thunder at the latest. You do not have to wait until play is officially suspended if you believe the situation to be dangerous.

Leave your golfing equipment behind and seek shelter
in the clubhouse
in a lightning shelter (leave equipment outside!)
in a car (not in a golf cart!)
in a dip/ hollow*
in an emergency in a dense wood*, but away from tree trunks.
* crouch down, with feet together

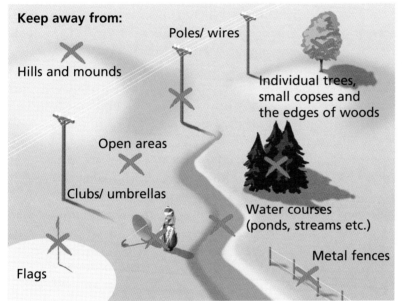

Keep away from:
Poles/ wires
Hills and mounds
Individual trees, small copses and the edges of woods
Open areas
Clubs/ umbrellas
Water courses (ponds, streams etc.)
Metal fences
Flags

Conduct if there is a risk of lightning. *Because of their metal equipment, golfers are particularly at risk in the event of lightning. Therefore, if a thunder storm is approaching, you should leave your equipment behind and find shelter in good time. Bear in mind that, as a player, you do not have to wait until play is officially suspended if you believe the situation to be dangerous, and that you are allowed to discontinue your round before that.*

It is advisable to only resume play 30 minutes after the last clap of thunder, at the earliest.

Instructions. Always heed the instructions and signs positioned around the golf course.

Children and pets. Neither small children nor dogs are usually allowed on the driving range or the golf course.

Mobile telephones. The use of mobile phones on the golf course is strictly forbidden in practically all clubs. They should also not be used in the clubhouse or on the driving range (an exception is made for doctors and those on emergency duty). However it is advisable to take your mobile phone (switched off) with you on the round in order to be able to call for help quickly in the event of emergencies or accidents.

8.8. Equipment

Completeness. Ensure that your equipment is in compliance with the rules and etiquette, and is complete.

Clothing. Please bear in mind that golf courses across the world have widely varying dress codes. This ranges from public courses without any stipulations (there is even a nudist golf course) to extremely traditional clubs which do not even allow short trousers, or only in combination with knee-length socks. The recommendations below contain practical advice and if you follow them it is unlikely that you will experience any problems.

When wearing shorts please ensure that they are not too short (some clubs even give very precise specifications on the length of shorts and stipulate that they are not to end more than a hand's width above the knee). Swimwear, tennis shorts and jogging trousers are to be avoided at all costs and blue jeans are also forbidden on practically all courses. As far as tops are concerned it is important that the shoulders are covered (e.g. no straps). Sleeveless blouses are usually only permitted if they have a collar. Men, on the other hand, are always to wear a polo shirt (with a collar), t-shirts are not permitted; shirts are to be tucked into the trousers.

Caps worn with the brim facing backwards are not approved of on some courses. Golf shoes are always to be worn, however please note that nailed shoes are now not allowed on most golf courses; softspikes are recommended.

For evenings, smart-casual clothing is usually appropriate if no other stipulations have been made. If you are not sure it is always wise to bring a jacket and a tie just in case.

Balls. The traditional colour for balls is white—coloured balls are not welcome on all courses. Playing on the course with driving range balls is strictly forbidden.

Separate equipment. It is forbidden for two players to play with one golf bag only (exception—if you are playing one ball together as a team one shared bag is allowed).

The dress code *expects women not to wear clothing which is too revealing and men not to wear collarless shirts. Shorts should be of an appropriate length (Bermuda shorts). Gary Player, one of the greatest golfers of all time, once said, "In addition to having proper clubs and balls, I feel that to play his best golf a golfer must feel well-dressed." A comment which can be agreed with whole-heartedly.*

Not appropriate *on most courses are strappy tops and, for men, collarless shirts. Short shorts, swimwear, track suits etc. should not be worn. Blue jeans are usually banned.*

8.9. Thoughtfulness with respect to women golfers

Ladies' golf. Although it is now difficult to believe, in days gone by there were some clubhouses which sported signs saying "Dogs and women not allowed"! Of course, in this day and age women are welcome in all golf clubs, but the custom of "ladies first" is still not applied on the teeing ground, albeit for a very good reason.

This often leads to a particularly unpleasant situation when individual ladies play a round of golf with several men. The men tee-off, walk ahead and almost forget to stop and wait quietly at the ladies' tee. It is then the lady's turn and the men walk on again immediately after she has played her stroke. The lady watches her ball land, picks up her tee and puts her club back in her bag. She then strolls after the men on her own. By the time she has reached her ball the men are often already waiting impatiently and the woman feels under pressure.

Therefore a plea to the men—keep your impatience in check and actually play golf *together* with the ladies by walking down the course together. It would be a shame if women only turned up to play golf on Ladies' Day.

Ladies' golf. The custom of "ladies first" does not apply to the golf course. This is all the more reason for the men to remember to wait quietly at the ladies' tee and walk down the course together with the female golfers in their group. After all, golf is supposed to be the sport of gentlemen.

6. Basic terminology

Abnormal ground conditions. This term includes three different conditions: *casual water, ground under repair* and certain *animal tracks* (see relevant section). The player is usually entitled to relief WITHOUT PENALTY from abnormal ground conditions.

Addressing the ball. A ball is classed as having been addressed when the player has taken his stance (i.e. has positioned his feet ready for a stroke) and has grounded the club. Please note: In *hazards* (bunkers and water hazards) the ball is considered to have been addressed as soon as the player has taken his *stance*—as he is not allowed to ground his club in these areas.

Advice. Advice is any guidance which would be helpful to the player and which might influence the stroke, the method of play or the choice of club. Requesting or giving advice is not allowed (except from a team partner when playing in a team competition or the caddie). Information which is available to everyone, such as the length of the hole, the location of hazards, the pin position etc., is not covered by this term.

Animal tracks. Certain animal tracks fall under the generic term "abnormal ground conditions". However it covers only three types of tracks, i.e. holes, casts and paths. A further stipulation is that these tracks have to be caused by burrowing animals, reptiles or birds (e.g. molehills, mouse holes, rabbit burrows and fox dens). As it is usually impossible to identify the tracks beyond doubt, this rule does not play an important role in actual golfing situations.

Ball. In competitions, only those balls which comply with the specifications in the rules are permitted. Practically all the products available in the shops fulfil these requirements. However care is to be taken when the conditions of competition demand balls which are included in the USGA's or R&A's "List of Conforming Golf Balls". If this is the case so-called X-out balls from approved brands (i.e. balls on which the brand name has been crossed out by a series of Xs) are, for example, not permitted. Driving range balls are only to be used on the practice ground.

In principal, the ball used to tee-off with must also be used to hole-out with at the hole being played. Therefore balls can only be changed between holes. However if a ball becomes unfit for play (deep grooves or other serious damage—simple scratches do not apply) during a hole, it can be replaced WITHOUT PENALTY after a fellow-competitor has been informed.

Bunker. A bunker is a hazard in the form of an area of ground which has been hollowed out and filled with sand. Grass-covered areas in the bunker are not a part of the bunker itself and are classed as being "through the green". A bunker running along the side of the fairway is called a fairway bunker and those around the green are termed greenside bunkers. (Bunker-like hollows, which are not filled with sand, can often be found on the course. They only consist of grass and are therefore sometimes referred to as grass bunkers. However they are not bunkers in the true sense of the word.)

Caddie. Caddie is the name given to the person who carries a player's clubs or passes them to him or who helps him in any other way in accordance with the rules.

The caddie "belongs" to the player—the latter being *responsible* for the former. If the caddie breaches a rule the player is penalised.

Casual water. Casual water is any area on the course, except for water hazards, where water has temporarily collected and which appears on the surface before or after the player has taken his stance (e.g. puddles of water, ice, snow). Casual water comes under the generic term "abnormal ground conditions".

Club-length. Unit of measure in golf whereby any club desired can be used to measure out the distance (the rules do allow extra long, so-called broom handle putters but they are not used for reasons of fairness).

NB: 1 club-length is used in the event of a drop WITHOUT PENALTY. However if a PENALTY OF 1 STROKE is given 2 club-lengths are usually measured.

Course. The entire area within which play can take place (i.e. excluding out of bounds).

Dropping. Dropping means to let the ball drop from shoulder height with the arm stretched horizontally. You are always permitted to clean a ball which is to be dropped.

The dropped ball is not allowed to
- roll into a hazard if it was dropped outside it,
- roll out of a hazard if it was dropped inside it,
- roll onto the green,
- roll out of bounds,
- roll back to the obstructed lie if relief has been taken from abnormal ground conditions or an immovable obstruction,
- roll more than two club-lengths from the point where it hit the ground after being dropped,
- roll nearer to the hole,
- hit the player or his equipment.

If one of the above happens the ball must be dropped again WITHOUT PENALTY. If one of the above occurs when the ball is dropped for a second time it must be placed on the spot where it hit the ground when it was dropped for the second time*. If the ball does not stay in position after being placed it must be placed again. If it still does not stay in position it is to be placed at the nearest point where it stays in position, not closer to the hole. (*Exception—if the ball hits the player or his equipment it cannot be placed even after it has been dropped for a second time and must be redropped until it no longer hits the player or his equipment.)

NB: To avoid misunderstandings and mix ups it is advisable to announce each new ball which is brought into play with its brand and number.

Equipment. The equipment consists of practically all the items belonging to a player. Small objects, such as coins, tees etc., which are used for marking, are not included.

Fairway. Closely-mown playing area. According to the rules the fairway is classed as being "through the green".

Fellow-competitor. Fellow-player in stroke play.

Basic terminology

Fringe. The fringe forms an intermediate stage between the fairway and the green. Despite the fact that the fringe is very similar to the green, according to the rules it does not belong to it but is classed as "through the green".

Green. The green is the name given to the low-cut area of grass around the hole which undergoes special preparation. This area is where putts are taken. The green requires the greatest amount of care possible.

Ground under repair (GUR). Ground under repair is any area on the course which has been declared as such by the Committee. GUR is marked in blue (stakes, lines etc.) or is explicitly defined in the Local Rules. Material piled up for removal and holes made by greenkeepers are also classed as ground under repair even if they are not marked or mentioned explicitly. Ground under repair comes under the generic term "abnormal ground conditions".

Hazard. Bunkers and water hazards are classed as hazards.

Honour. The player who is entitled to play his tee shot first is said to have the honour. The honour should not be declined.

Lift, clean, place. See "Preferred lies".

Line of play. The line which the player intends the ball to take after a stroke (only as far as the hole but with an appropriate distance each side of the line). Compare with "Line of putt".

Line of putt. The line which the player intends the ball to take after a stroke played on the *green* (only as far as the hole but with an appropriate distance each side of the line). Compare with "Line of play".

Local Rules. The Local Rules are drawn up separately for each golf course. They can be found on the back of the score card or on the notice board.

Loose impediments. This term covers all natural objects, such as stones, leaves, twigs, branches, dung, worms and insects as well as their casts, if the objects concerned are loose i.e. they are not fixed, growing, firmly embedded and do not stick to the ball. Loose impediments can be removed WITHOUT PENALTY on the entire course, except in hazards.

NB: Dew and frost are not covered by this term. Sand and loose soil are only classed as loose impediments when they are on the *green.*

Lost ball. According to the rules a ball is lost if it is out of bounds, if it cannot be found within 5 minutes or cannot be identified as the player's own. The player has to go back to the place where the last stroke was taken from and take a drop under PENALTY OF 1 STROKE (tee-up on the teeing ground).

Marker. The marker (also called scorer) is the person who records the number of strokes for a player. The marker is not the player's referee and therefore does not have any decision-making powers. This term is also often used to refer to the ball-marker (see below).

Marking. Marking a ball means to denote its position. A special ball-marker is the ideal tool for this on the green. It has a short shaft and a flat surface. A coin or, if nothing else is available, a removable button, which can be found on any golf glove, are also often used. Off the green, it is advisable to use a larger object, such as a tee or a pitch repairer.

Match play. In match play direct opponents play against each other on a hole by hole basis. The winner is the player who leads by more holes than are still left to play. Special match play rules apply to this form of competition (see page 156ff.).

NB: If there are no other stipulations to the contrary, the penalty for breaching the rules in match play is LOSING THE HOLE.

Moved ball. A ball is deemed to have moved if it starts to move and then comes to rest in a different position i.e. its location changes. Therefore if the ball merely rocks or wobbles it is not classed as having moved as defined by the rules.

Mulligan. The "Mulligan" is a popular custom on the first tee which, however, is not provided for in the rules. It involves giving the player a "free" second attempt if he mishits his first shot—without counting the first stroke or a penalty stroke. This form of relief can only be given on private, friendly rounds.

Nearest point of relief. In numerous relief procedures the ball is to be dropped at the nearest point where the interference no longer exists.

Please note that this point is not permitted to be nearer to the hole than the ball's original position. Furthermore, the player cannot drop from one area into another without penalty, i.e. if relief is taken in a bunker the ball *cannot* be dropped outside of the bunker without penalty. The same applies to water hazards.

Obstruction. Everything on the course which is artificial is classed as an obstruction, including the artificially laid surfaces of roads and paths. Obstructions do not belong to the game of golf in the true sense therefore relief WITHOUT PENALTY can be taken from them in most cases. However the Committee can declare artificial objects to be an integral part of the course—they are then no longer an obstruction and relief WITHOUT PENALTY IS NOT given. There are movable obstructions and immovable obstructions.

NB: Objects which define out of bounds (posts, fences, walls etc.) are never classed as obstructions.

Order of play. At the first tee the order of play is determined by the line up (list of tee times). If this is not available lots are drawn. In private, friendly rounds it is customary to start in accordance with handicap, whereby the player with the lowest handicap has the honour.

On the following tees the person who had the best result at the previous hole has the honour. However if a player plays from the back tees he usually tees-off before all the players teeing-off in front of him.

After the tee shots it is always the player's turn whose ball is the furthest away from the hole. In the interests of saving time this order may be deviated from (for example, especially if a ball comes to rest extremely close to the hole).

Out of bounds (OB). Out of bounds refers to the areas which, according to the rules, are not part of the course. A ball that is out of bounds is not to be played under any circumstances (return to the site of the last stroke and take a drop/ tee-up on the teeing ground, UNDER PENALTY OF 1 STROKE). Out of bounds is usually marked in white (posts, fences, walls etc.), however sometimes it is not marked with a colour and is only stipulated in the Local Rules.

Outside agency. Anything which does not belong to the player himself or to his equipment (e.g. animals, walkers, other players etc.).
NB: However wind and rain are not outside agencies. This means that if a ball is moved or diverted by wind or rain it must be played as it lies.

Penalty stroke. A penalty stroke is not a stroke played in the true sense. It is a stroke which must be added to the score due to a playing error or to a breach of the rules.
NB: 1 PENALTY STROKE is usually applied in the event of a playing error (ball in the water, out of bounds etc.) and 2 PENALTY STROKES are the result of a breach of the rules which could have been avoided if more care had been taken (club grounded in the bunker, ball hits player's own equipment etc.).

Pitch mark/ repairer. Holes which are caused when the ball hits the green are termed pitch marks. The tool used to fix these marks is called a pitch repairer. Every golfer should have a pitch repairer in his bag at all times.

Practice stroke/ swing. A practice stroke involves hitting a ball for practice purposes. In contrast, a practice swing is merely a swing movement without attempting to hit the ball. It is therefore an intentional air shot for the purpose of developing a feeling for a stroke.
Practice strokes are generally not permitted during a round. However practice swings can be carried out at any time if a rule is not breached in doing so (in hazards in particular one must bear in mind that the club is not permitted to touch the ground).

Basic terminology

Preferred lies. During the winter, or when the course is in poor condition, the Committee can allow preferred lies by way of exception (also known as "winter rules" or "lift, clean, place"). The ball's lie can then be marked and the ball can be picked up and cleaned. It must then be put back within one score card length (sometimes within one club-length) of the original lie, not nearer to the hole.

Provisional ball. A provisional ball is played if the original ball could be "lost", i.e. there is a possibility that it has landed out of bounds or that it cannot be found. A provisional ball is played to save time.

Reading. Reading the green means examining and assessing it, using your eyes only, with respect to the turf conditions and gradients in order to determine the ideal line of putt. Reading the green is to be distinguished from testing its surface by roughening the grass or rolling a ball, which is not permitted.

Relief. The player has a right to relief (without penalty) under certain circumstances which are precisely defined in the rules. The use of a relief procedure is usually optional but can be prescribed by the Local Rules in certain cases. If relief is not explicitly provided for by the rules the principle of playing the ball as it lies applies.

Rough. Long or uncut grass, bushes and wooded areas. According to the rules the rough is classed as being "through the green".

Rub of the green. If a ball in motion is accidentally diverted by an external factor this is considered a rub of the green and the ball must usually be played as it lies.

Semi-rough. An intermediate stage between the fairway and the rough. According to the rules the semi-rough is classed as being through the green.

Stroke. The stroke is defined as the forward movement of the club with the intention of hitting the ball. Therefore a mishit or a stroke which misses the ball completely (so-called air shot) also count. The rules require a genuine stroke—other ways of moving the ball, e.g. prodding, pushing, spooning up, scraping etc. are not permitted.

Stroke play. In stroke play, the winner is the player who required the least number of strokes for the round.
NB: If there are no other stipulations to the contrary, the penalty for breaching the rules in stroke play is 2 PENALTY STROKES.

Tee. The tee is the wooden/ plastic pin on which the ball is placed for the tee shot. This term is also often used to refer to the teeing ground.

Teeing ground. The teeing ground is usually slightly raised and is made up of a level, rectangular, closely-mown area of grass. It is the starting point of the hole to be played. In order to do justice to different golfing abilities each hole has several teeing grounds which are marked with different colours.

Tee shot. The tee shot is the stroke made from the teeing ground.

Tending. Tending the flag refers to when a person determined by the player holds the flag and removes it straight after the shot. The person tending the flag should stand at the side of the hole, holding the flag with his arm stretched out horizontally.

Testing. Testing the surface of a green by *roughening the grass* or *rolling a ball* is not permitted. Compare with "Reading".

Through the green. The term "through the green" refers to the entire area of the course, excluding out of bounds, the teeing ground and the green of the hole to be played as well as all hazards.

Unplayable ball. A ball can be declared unplayable at any time and anywhere on the course, *except for in water hazards.* Whether the ball, objectively speaking, really is in an unplayable position is irrelevant. Every player is completely free to decide whether to declare his ball unplayable and to take a drop under PENALTY OF 1 STROKE.

Water hazard. Water hazards are natural or artificially created watercourses (rivers, ponds, lakes, the sea etc.). Regular water hazards are marked with yellow stakes, lateral water hazards are marked with red stakes.

NB: The official rules do not use the term "regular" but only differentiate between water hazards and lateral water hazards. However the term is used throughout this book as it makes it easier to distinguish between the two types of water hazard.

Winter rules. See "Preferred lies".

III. Practical section

1. Before entering the golf club

Visitors. If you intend to play at a club which is not your home club it is advisable to call in advance and inquire whether guests are welcome and whether a handicap certificate is required. In some clubs, especially in European countries, guests are only ever permitted on weekdays and a minimum handicap of 30 or less is often required. In certain private clubs guests are only ever allowed to play if they are accompanied by a member.

Starting time. Always ring the club to check whether the course is at all playable (it could be closed due to bad weather conditions or because of a competition) and to reserve a starting time if necessary.
If you are taking part in a competition you can usually find out your starting time by calling the secretary's office the day before the event. This information is also sometimes available on the internet.

Equipment. Check to make sure you have packed all important items. Small items, such as tees, balls etc. can be bought at the pro shop if necessary.

Inner calmness. Allow yourself plenty of time when going to play golf. If you are under stress, tired or in a hurry, or if you are preoccupied by personal problems or unfinished work, you will probably not be able to play to the standard you would like.

Time in hand. It is advisable to arrive at the golf club at least an hour before your tee-off time. It is only then that you will have enough time to check your equipment, to get changed, to deal with administrative issues, to warm up on the driving range and to be standing ready on the first tee 10 minutes before your tee-off time.

2. In the clubhouse

Registration and payment. Upon arrival at the golf club you should register immediately in the pro shop or the secretary's office. Some clubs like to keep a record of the visitors playing their course. If so, you should enter your name and all the required information in their guest book. Do not forget to take enough loose change/ tokens for the ball machine at the driving range and pay the fees due:

• **Range fee**
  Fee for using the driving range.

• **Green fee**
  Fee for playing on the golf course (either for 18 holes or for a day) incl. range fee.

• **Match fee**
  Start/ entry fee for competitions.

• **Trolley fee**
  Fee to hire a golf trolley.

• **Cart fee**
  Fee to hire a golf cart.

Changing rooms. In practically every golf club changing rooms are provided in the clubhouse for players and visitors. Please also use these rooms (rather than the car park) to change your shoes. Please bear in mind that there could be sections of the clubhouse which are reserved for members only.

Score card. If you are about to play in a competition always check your score card. It is especially important to check whether the *handicap* recorded is your current one. If this is not the case clarify the discrepancy with the Committee immediately. (In particular do not put it off until after the round as this would be more than four hours later and you would probably have forgotten about it by then. A player who hands in a score card with a handicap which is too high will be disqualified[1].)

Marker	Hole	Men champion	Men medal	Ladies champion	Ladies medal	Hcp	Par	Player			+ 0 -
Player: Jeff Miller						Hcp: 19.8/24					
Competition: Audi Quattro Cup Stableford/ back tees						Date: 10.07.04					
	1	380	345	335	315	7	4				
	2	370	350	315	295	9	4				
	3	490	475	445	420	15	5				
	4	175	160	155	140	11	3				
	5	325	275	270	235	17	4				
	6	560	520	495	460	3	5				
	7	195	170	165	145	13	3				
	8	400	385	355	340	1	4				

Form and conditions of play. Find out about the form of play for the competition (e.g. Stableford, stroke play, match play etc.), about the tees which you are to play from (which colour) and the number of the hole you are to start from.
Read the *Local Rules* on the back of the score card or on the notice board. Also watch out for notices concerning *temporary rules* and *conditions of competition.*

Golf carts. If you are going to use a golf cart read the relevant safety stipulations and traffic regulations carefully. As golf carts could damage the grass, driving them on the fairway is often prohibited. Banning these vehicles from leaving the paths is common practice and one must walk from there to the ball. However, driving on the fairway is sometimes allowed—whereby the distance is to be kept as short as possible, i.e. you drive along the cart paths until you are level with the ball and then drive to the ball at an angle of 90° (90° cart rule).

Equipment. Double-check your equipment—any missing items can be purchased at the pro shop.

In the clubhouse

☑ **Equipment checklist**

☐ Membership badge or green fee card (well visible)
☐ Score card and pencil/ waterproof pen
☐ Clubs (max. 14)
☐ Bag, trolley if required
☐ Shoes
☐ Gloves
☐ Balls (in sufficient quantity)
☐ Tees (in sufficient quantity)
☐ Ball-marker
☐ Pitch repairer
☐ Cloth for cleaning the clubs and the ball
☐ Umbrella/ waterproof clothing, rain cover for the bag
☐ Hat/ cap/ visors, sun cream
☐ Food/ drinks
☐ Ashtray for smokers
☐ Rule book/ "Golf Rules Quick Reference Guide"
☐ ....
☐ ....

1 Rule 6-2.b.

3. On the driving range

Consideration and safety. When arriving at the range please avoid disturbing the players who are practicing. Try not to enter into discussions or only talk very quietly so as not to break other players' concentration. For your own safety keep well clear of players who are holding a club or who look like they are going to play a stroke.

Care. Please observe the instructions concerning the teeing grounds—especially the fact that teeing-off from the grass is only allowed where it is expressly permitted (this area is usually indicated by two ropes). Divots are not to be replaced on the driving range.

Tee-off area. On the driving range please only tee-off from the mats or between the ropes. However be careful not to tee-off too near to the ropes—when playing a shot your club could get caught up in the rope, causing injury to yourself.

Preventing accidents. Bear in mind that players stand relatively close to each other on a driving range and therefore there is an increased risk of accidents. Most injuries occur when a person is standing within the swing radius of another player.
Always stay at the same level as the other players and do not, under any circumstances, walk on the target area of the driving range while it is in use (especially not to collect balls or tees which have flown off). You should also never walk onto the target area from any holes which border it (the driving range is usually classed as out of bounds in these cases anyway).

On the driving range

Ensure that the target area is free. Check that no greenkeepers are working in the target area. Also pay particular attention to people who are playing on fairways which border onto the driving range.

Break. If you take a break while practicing on the driving range please free the teeing ground for another player and take your equipment with you.

Practice green and bunker. The putting green is usually intended exclusively for holing-out with the putter. A special chipping/ pitching green is provided for chipping (short, low approach shots) or pitching (short, high approach shots). Out of courtesy to following players marks in the practice bunker should be smoothed out after the practice session.

Driving range balls. The practice balls are the property of the driving range and are *never* to be removed from the premises. The driving range fee only includes the hire of the balls.

__Driving range balls__ are only to be used on the driving range and not on the course under any circumstances. This may be penalised with being barred from the course.

Ball buckets. Please return empty ball buckets to the ball machine.

4. Important basic rules

Principle—playing the ball as it lies. If a rule does not expressly allow anything else, the basic principle of the game of golf says that

- the ball should not be touched in between the tee and the green[1],
- the ball should be played as it lies (or if its lie has been changed it should be played as it lay when it came to rest)[2],
- the course should be played as you find it[3].

This includes that you should never attempt to gain an unfair advantage by improving the lie of the ball, the area of the intended stance and swing or the line of play in an *unjustified* manner (this also applies to the area where a ball is to be dropped or placed). In particular you are not permitted to *move, bend or break* off anything growing or fixed (e.g. breaking off branches, levelling out unevenness in the ground etc.) before making a stroke[4].

This basic principle can only be deviated from if a rule provides for a relief procedure and *expressly* permits something else. If in doubt you are well-advised to simply play the ball as it lies[5]. In doing so it is practically impossible to do anything wrong unless the ball is

- out of bounds[6],
- on the wrong green[7],
- in an area where playing is not permitted as stated in the Local Rules[8] (e.g. GUR, environmentally-sensitive area).

If it is not at all possible to play the ball as it lies you can, of course, also declare it unplayable[9] or proceed in accordance with the rule governing water hazards[10]—then, however, incurring 1 PENALTY STROKE.

In particular, the ball is also to be played as it lies if the player is unhappy with the result of his shot, e.g. because he was distracted by a car driving past, a fellow-competitor sneezing etc. Distractions are a part of the game[11] and in golf you virtually never have the chance to replay a shot without incurring a penalty of some kind.

Important basic rules

If you observe this basic principle you will hardly ever fall foul of the rules. Furthermore, never attempt to circumvent a rule or to bend it to your advantage as the rules have made provision for this type of conduct as well[12]. In contrast to most sets of laws, the rules of golf are practically watertight.

Procedure to be followed if in doubt about the rules. If you find yourself in a situation where you are unsure about the correct action to take, discuss the problem with your fellow-competitors. However, please bear in mind that your fellow-competitors, especially your marker, are *not* authorised to make decisions. If you act on rules information provided by a fellow-competitor which then turns out to be incorrect, you, as the player, will carry the sole responsibility for this mistake. If necessary, also refer to a rule book (if you have a copy of "Golf Rules Quick Reference Guide" with you, this practical booklet should help you to find the answer to most questions very quickly, see page 164f.).

If, after consulting your fellow-players and the rule book, you are still in doubt about the correct action to take you can then play a second ball[13]. In doing so, it is important that you inform your fellow-competitors which of the two balls played are to count in the event that both variants conform with the rules. After completing the round you are to clarify the matter with the Committee and you can then enter the right number of strokes on the score card[14].

An example. Your ball has become embedded near the green. While you are aware that you are given FREE RELIEF from balls which have become embedded into closely-mown areas[15], in this case you cannot tell whether or not the area involved is actually a "closely-mown" area in accordance with the rules. Announce that, to be on the safe side, you are going to play two balls and also which of the two will count, e.g. the ball which is played under application of the relief procedure if this conforms with the rules.

1. Play the original ball as it lies by hacking it out of its embedded lie as best as you can.
2. Take relief WITHOUT PENALTY by dropping a second ball next to the pitch-mark and playing from there.

Play both balls into the hole and note down both scores for the two variants. Clarify the matter after completion of the round with the Committee.

Dishonesty. Players who agree not to apply a rule or to waive a penalty will be DISQUALIFIED[16].
Players who try to influence the lie or the movement of a ball in a way not provided for in the rules will incur 2 PENALTY STROKES or, in serious cases, will be DISQUALIFIED[17].
Playing outside the correct order of play is permitted and is sometimes even necessary in order to save time. However if the players have agreed upon the wrong order of play to gain a *tactical advantage* they will be DISQUALIFIED[18].

Clubs. The clubs must comply with certain specifications as provided for in the rules of golf, otherwise the player will be DISQUALIFIED[19]. Therefore it is advisable not to try to make changes to your golf clubs yourself.
A player is allowed to carry a maximum of 14 clubs around the course. If a player is inadvertently carrying more than this number of clubs he will incur 2 PENALTY STROKES for each hole on which he had too many clubs, to a maximum of 4 PENALTY STROKES for a round[20].
You are not permitted to borrow a club from another player on the course in order to play a stroke with it[21].

Ball. The penalty for playing a ball which is not permitted by the rules is disqualification[22]. If you are playing in a tournament, please follow the instructions in the conditions of competition as they could contain more detailed regulations concerning balls to be used[23].

Golf balls. *If playing in a tournament, please pay attention to the conditions of competition—sometimes particular balls are specified in it and, for example, so-called X-out balls are not permitted.*
Damaged balls can be swapped at any time.

It is a principle of the game of golf that the ball which is used to tee-off with should also be used to hole-out with on the hole being played[24]; therefore balls can only be swapped *between* holes. However if a ball becomes *unfit for play* (deep cuts or other serious damage—simple scratches do not apply) during a hole, it can be swapped WITHOUT PENALTY. However a fellow-player has to be informed of this in advance to give him the opportunity to observe the procedure[25].

Practicing on the course. Practicing on the competition course is not permitted *before the round* on the day of a *stroke play* competition. If a competition takes place over several rounds on consecutive days, practicing *between rounds* is also not permitted on the course which will be used in the coming days. Even testing the surface of a green (by means of practice putts, rolling the ball or roughening or scraping the surface) is forbidden before the round, under penalty of DISQUALIFICATION[26].

During the round the surface of a green is also not to be tested[27], nor is practicing allowed[28]—the penalty incurred in this case is 2 STROKES. (An exception to this is that chipping and putting is allowed between holes either on the green played last or on the next tee[29].)

NB: A practice *swing* is not a practice stroke and can be taken at any time if this does not involve breaching a rule[30] (e.g. touching the ground in a hazard).

Advice. In golf, each player is basically left to their own devices. Players who, during the round, *request* instruction from their fellow-competitors or onlookers in the form of advice are given 2 PENALTY STROKES[31]. This also applies to *giving* advice. However, requesting and providing information which is *generally available* is permitted—this includes instruction on the rules, the location of hazards or pin positions[32].

Naturally, a player who is given unsolicited advice does NOT INCUR ANY PENALTY STROKES.

On the other hand, if you are involved in a team competition you are allowed to consult your team partner at any time. This also applies if you are playing with a caddie—after all, that is exactly what he is there for[33].

Caddie. Please bear in mind that, as a player, you are responsible for all actions made by your caddie. If your caddie breaches a rule you will incur the penalty as the player[34]. Furthermore, the main function of the caddie is to carry the player's clubs and to provide him with support in an *advisory* capacity. Under no circumstances is he allowed to provide *physical* support *while* the player is playing a stroke e.g. by letting the player lean on him, holding branches to the side or protecting him from the elements[35].

No protection from the elements. Nowhere on the course is the player entitled to be protected from the elements (e.g. strong wind, dazzling sun, torrential rain) by a third party while playing a stroke.

Delaying and discontinuing play. Players who play too slowly incur 2 PENALTY STROKES—if this conduct is repeated they can even be DISQUALIFIED[36]. Discontinuing play without authorisation[37] or leaving the assigned group[38] is also punished with DISQUALIFICATION.

However if the players have a valid reason, e.g. illness, accident, darkness or risk of lightning (heavy rain in itself is not a valid reason) they definitely are allowed to discontinue play[39]. In particular, please bear in mind that in the event of a thunder storm involving lightning you do not have to wait for an official discontinuation, you can make the decision on your own initiative if you believe the situation to be dangerous.

If the Committee has temporarily suspended play you *have to* stop playing (although any holes that have been started can be played to the end)[40]. In this case the ball can be marked and picked up[41].

Lifting the ball and placing/ dropping it. As mentioned earlier (see page 67), while a hole is being played the ball is, in principle, not to be touched again until the green has been reached[42]. Therefore, in order to avoid any possible misunderstandings, it is advisable to inform the marker or another fellow-competitor in advance each time a ball is picked up in accordance with the rules (in order to take relief of some form or for any other authorised course of action) and give him the opportunity to observe the procedure.

If a ball is to be *put back* after a particular procedure, it is imperative that its position is marked prior to picking it up[43]. To do this it is preferable to use a ball-marker or a coin on the green and a slightly bigger object such as a tee or a pitch repairer off the green.

However if a ball is to be *dropped* within the framework of a particular rule it is not imperative that its position is marked before doing so[44]—it is, nevertheless, advisable. A ball which is to be *dropped* can always be cleaned[45].

Dropping means to let a ball drop from shoulder height with the arm stretched horizontally[46].

***Dropping.** When dropping a ball the player must stand upright and let the ball drop with his arm stretched out horizontally at shoulder height. You are, however, definitely allowed to look where you are dropping the ball and to aim at the most favourable spot within the area specified by the rules.*

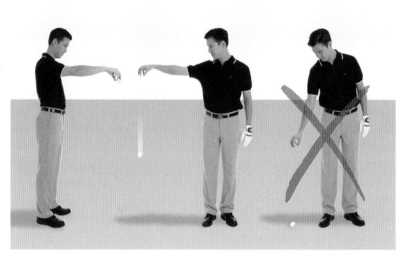

When dropping a ball it must be ensured that it does *not* come to rest in certain particular positions. If one of the following cases occurs the ball must be dropped for a second time WITHOUT PENALTY[47].

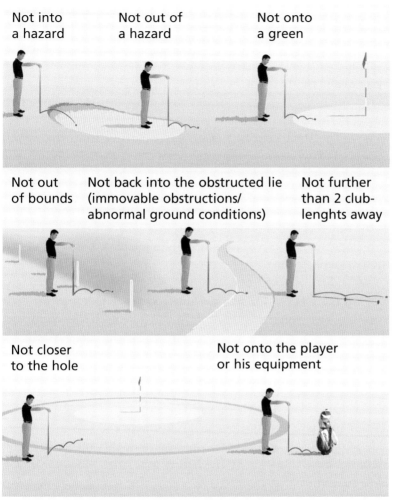

Not into a hazard

Not out of a hazard

Not onto a green

Not out of bounds

Not back into the obstructed lie (immovable obstructions/ abnormal ground conditions)

Not further than 2 club-lenghts away

Not closer to the hole

Not onto the player or his equipment

Eight situations which are not to occur when a ball is dropped. But there is no cause for concern, you do not necessarily have to learn all of these eight situations off by heart. If one of the first five situations occurs it will usually be obvious to you that there is a problem. Only the last three situations are to be committed to memory as, if they occur, you might not always automatically realise that a rule has been breached.

If one of the above situations occurs again when the ball is dropped for a second time it must be placed on the spot where it hit the ground when it was dropped for the second time[48].

Exception: If the ball hits the player or his equipment it cannot be placed even after it has been dropped for a second time, but must be dropped again and again[49].

If a ball does not stay in position after being placed it must be placed again. If it still does not stay in position it is to be placed at the nearest point where is does not move, not closer to the hole[50].

To avoid misunderstandings and mix-ups it is advisable to announce each new ball which is brought into play with the brand and the number.

Important basic rules

Playing from the wrong spot. If you have dropped or placed a ball in the wrong manner or on the wrong spot, but have *not yet played* the ball, you are allowed to pick the ball up WITHOUT PENALTY and proceed correctly[51].

However if the ball has been played, the stroke counts and the player incurs 1 PENALTY STROKE for dropping in an incorrect manner[52] or 2 PENALTY STROKES for playing from the wrong spot[53]. (The most common example of playing from the wrong spot is a ball which has been moved and then, mistakenly, has not been put back.) If, however, a player plays from the wrong spot thereby winning a *significant* advantage, with respect to distance or to any other gain, he will be DISQUALIFIED[54] (e.g. a player drops a ball which is out of bounds at the point where it crossed the out of bounds margin instead of returning to the place where he played his last stroke from).

Playing the wrong ball. In principle you are to hole-out with the same ball that you teed-off with[55]. If you play with the wrong ball during the course of a hole you are to rectify the mistake by going back up the course, looking for the correct ball and finishing the hole with it—the penalty for not doing so is DISQUALIFICATION[56].

If you have played with the wrong ball *in a bunker or a water hazard* and have not played any strokes with the wrong ball outside a hazard you will NOT INCUR ANY PENALTY STROKES[57] (as you are not allowed to identify the ball in a hazard). However, if you have played one or more strokes with the wrong ball *outside a hazard* you will incur 2 PENALTY STROKES[58]. Therefore it is advisable to get into the habit of taking a close look at the ball before playing each stroke to make sure that it is actually yours.

Ball interferes with or assists play. Every player is permitted to pick up his ball if he believes that it could assist another player's game[59] (e.g. by acting as a target or as a stopper).

He can also have another ball picked up if he believes that the ball could interfere with his game or help the game of another player[60].

Striking the ball more than once. If you accidentally strike the ball more than once when playing a shot, 1 PENALTY STROKE must be added to the stroke[61] (see illustration on page 107).

Ball at rest moved. The intention of the rules of golf are that the ball is to be played as it lies or, if its lie has been changed, as it lay when it came to rest. This means that if a ball *at rest* is moved by an external factor it has to be put back in its original position WITHOUT PENALTY[62].

- **Outside agency**
  If a ball at rest is moved by anything that is not part of the player's game (e.g. animals, walkers, other players etc.) the ball is to be put back WITHOUT PENALTY[63]. If the ball has even been picked up and taken away you are allowed to place a *new* ball on the spot where the original ball was lying, WITHOUT PENALTY[64].

- **Another ball**
  If a ball at rest is hit by another ball and is moved as a result this other ball can also be viewed as an outside agency and the ball which was moved is to be put back WITHOUT PENALTY[65].

- **Player or his equipment**
  If the ball at rest is moved unintentionally by the player himself or by his equipment he must put the ball back, however in this case under PENALTY OF 1 STROKE[66].

- **Wind and gravity**
  Wind and gravity are not classed as external factors, i.e. if the ball is moved by a gust of wind or moves by itself (without the player having addressed it) this is part of the game and the ball has to be played as it lies from its new position, WITHOUT PENALTY[67].

Moved   Not moved

Moved ball. A ball is deemed to have moved if its position changes. Therefore if the ball merely rocks or wobbles it is not classed as having moved in accordance with the rules.

Important basic rules

Ball in motion deflected or stopped. If a ball *in motion* is deflected or stopped by an external factor this is considered a rub of the green and the ball is normally to be played as it lies[68] (after all nobody can tell where the ball would have ended up if the incident had not occurred).

- **Outside agency**
  If a ball in motion is deflected or stopped by anything which is not part of the player's game (spectator, fellow-player etc.) this is considered a rub of the green and the ball is normally to be played as it lies, WITHOUT PENALTY[63]. (Except for on the green where the shot is usually to be repeated WITHOUT PENALTY[70]).

- **Another ball**
  If a ball hits another ball it is usually also to be played as it lies WITHOUT PENALTY[71]. (Except for on the green—if both balls were on the green before the stroke was played the player usually incurs 2 PENALTY STROKES[72].)

- **Player or his equipment**
  If a ball hits the player himself or his equipment he must play the ball as it lies under PENALTY OF 2 STROKES[73] (therefore you should be careful never to leave your golf bag or cart in the line of play).

- **Rain and storms**
  If a ball is deflected by the wind or by rain this can also be viewed as a rub of the green and the player is simply to continue to play the ball as it lies[74].

- **Flagstick**
  If the ball hits the untended flagstick in the hole, after being played from off the green, this is classed as a rub of the green and the ball is to be played as it lies, WITHOUT PENALTY[75].
  However if the ball hits the flagstick after being played from on the green the player incurs 2 PENALTY STROKES[76].

NB: The situations described clearly illustrate that the player is only penalised in cases where the blame lies with the player himself, i.e. he could have easily prevented the ball from being moved or deflected if he had taken a little more care.

Ball at rest is moved ...

	by the player himself or his equipment	put the ball back	normally with 1 penalty stroke*
	by an outside agency	put the ball back	without penalty
	by another ball	put the ball back	without penalty
	by the wind or on its own	play the ball as it lies	without penalty

*Without penalty when looking for a ball in abnormal ground conditions (GUR, casual water, certain animal tracks), when removing movable obstructions, and on the green when removing loose impediments or in the process of marking, lifting or putting back the ball.

Ball at rest moved. If a ball at rest is moved it usually has to be put back in its original position. If the movement was caused by the player himself he usually incurs 1 penalty stroke.

Ball in motion hits ...

	the player or his equipment	play the ball as it lies	2 penalty strokes
	an outside agency	normally play the ball as it lies*	without penalty
	another ball	play the ball as it lies	normally without penalty, exc. green**
	the flagstick	play the ball as it lies	normally without penalty, exc. green**

*If, after a stroke on the green, the ball hits something which moves or is alive, the stroke has to be repeated, without penalty.
**2 penalty strokes, if the ball hits another ball at rest on the green or the flagstick after a stroke on the green.

Moving ball deflected. If a ball in flight or a rolling ball hits something and is thereby deflected it is usually to be played as it lies. If the ball has hit the player himself or if the collision has been caused by his own carelessness, he usually incurs 2 penalty strokes.

Provisional ball. If you suspect that the ball could be "lost" (it could have landed out of bounds or you might not be able to find it), you should definitely play a provisional ball in order to save time[77]. This is because when a ball is lost the player usually has to play from the spot where the last stroke was taken from[78]. If this situation is foreseeable, playing a second, so-called provisional, ball saves the player from having to walk back—in the event that the original ball actually does turn out to be lost.

You always have the option of playing a provisional ball except if the ball has landed in a water hazard (then you must proceed in accordance with the water hazard rule, see page 122ff.). Do not be overly optimistic—it is far better to play a provisional ball one too many times than to risk having to walk all the way back again.

If you decide to play a provisional ball you have to do so *before* moving on and starting to look for the original ball. If you have already looked for the ball for a while and only then return to play a would-be provisional ball, this does not actually count as a provisional ball but is classed as a new ball in play—under PENALTY OF 1 STROKE[80].

Announce the provisional ball, loudly and clearly, as being "provisional", stating the brand and the number, and drop it as near as possible to the spot where the last stroke was played from. If this was the tee you are allowed to tee-up again[81].

If you do not explicitly announce that the second ball is "provisional" it also becomes the new ball in play under PENALTY OF 1 STROKE[82].

If there is a possibility that the provisional ball could also be lost another provisional ball can be played[83].

You are then allowed to play the provisional ball until you reach the approximate position where you believe the original ball to be[84].

• **Original ball found**
  If you find your original ball within 5 minutes and it is not out of bounds you *have to* continue play with it[85]. This applies even if the original ball is lying in a poor or practically unplayable position. The provisional ball has to be picked up. Strokes made with the provisional ball do not count and there are NO PENALTY STROKES for having played a provisional ball[86].

- **Original ball lost**
  If your original ball really is out of bounds or if you cannot find it within 5 minutes, the provisional ball becomes the ball in play with 1 PENALTY STROKE[87], i.e. all the strokes played with both the original ball and with the provisional ball count, plus 1 PENALTY STROKE.

- **Special case**
  The provisional ball also automatically becomes the ball in play under PENALTY OF 1 STROKE as soon as it is hit from a position which is nearer to the hole than where the original ball is believed to be[88].

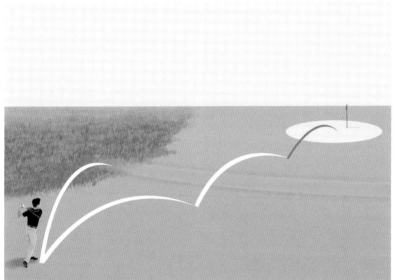

Provisional ball. You are allowed to play your provisional ball until you reach the approximate area where you believe your original ball to be. Your provisional ball is also allowed to go past this position however you are not allowed to play a stroke past this point if you want the ball to remain provisional. If you have played a shot such as this before finding the original ball the provisional ball automatically becomes the new ball in play under penalty of 1 stroke.

NB: The player never has the choice between 2 balls on the course. If he finds his original ball (within 5 minutes and on the course) he *has to* play it. If the provisional ball has a very good lie and you suspect that the original ball is in an very difficult position, it is therefore advisable to not even look for it in the first place and continue to play the provisional ball straight away.

Playing from the position of the last stroke (penalty of stroke and distance). An option which is *always* open to a player is to take a drop on the spot where the last stroke was played from (tee-up on the teeing ground), incurring 1 PENALTY STROKE[89].

Important basic rules

Provisional ball. At first sight, the provisional ball procedure appears to be rather complicated. However the flow chart opposite should make it easy to gain an overall picture of this procedure.

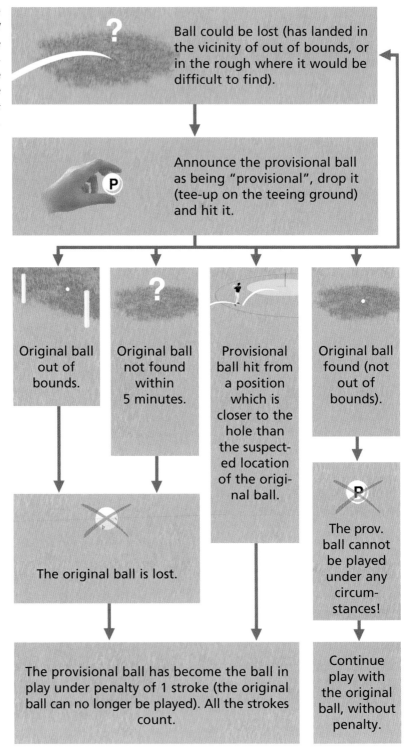

Ball could be lost (has landed in the vicinity of out of bounds, or in the rough where it would be difficult to find).

Announce the provisional ball as being "provisional", drop it (tee-up on the teeing ground) and hit it.

Original ball out of bounds.

Original ball not found within 5 minutes.

Provisional ball hit from a position which is closer to the hole than the suspected location of the original ball.

Original ball found (not out of bounds).

The original ball is lost.

The prov. ball cannot be played under any circumstances!

The provisional ball has become the ball in play under penalty of 1 stroke (the original ball can no longer be played). All the strokes count.

Continue play with the original ball, without penalty.

1 Rule 18-2.a.
2 Rule 13-1. in conj. with rule 18-1.
3 Rule 13.
4 Rule 13-2.
5 Rule 13-1.
6 Rule 27-1.
7 Rule 25-3.
8 Note 2 on definition of "ground under repair" and note 2 on definition of "water hazard".
9 Rule 28.
10 Rule 26.
11 Decision 1-4/1.
12 Rule 1-4.
13 Rule 3-3.a.
14 Rule 3-3.b.
15 Rule 25-2.
16 Rule 1-3.
17 Rule 1-2.
18 Rule 10-2.c.
19 Rule 4-1. to 3.
20 Rule 4-4.
21 Rule 4-4.a.
22 Rule 5-1.
23 Note on rule 5-1.
24 Rule 1-1. in conj. with rule 15-1.
25 Rule 5-3.
26 Rule 7-1.b.
27 Rule 16-1.d.
28 Rule 7-2.
29 Ibid.
30 Note 1 on rule 7.
31 Rule 8-1.
32 Definition of "advice".
33 Rule 8-1.b.
34 Rule 6-1.
35 Rule 14-2.a.
36 Rule 6-7.
37 Rule 6-8.a.
38 Rule 6-3.b.
39 Rule 6-8.a.
40 Rule 6-8.b.
41 Rule 6-8.c.
42 Rule 18-2.a.
43 Rule 20-1.
44 Argumentum e contrario, rule 20-1.
45 Rule 21.
46 Rule 20-2.a.
47 Rule 20-2.c.
48 Ibid.
49 Rule 20-2.a.
50 Rule 20-3.d.
51 Rule 20-6.
52 Rule 20-2.a.
53 Rule 20-7.c.
54 Ibid. and decision 20-7b/0.5.
55 Rule 15-1.
56 Rule 15-3.b.
57 Ibid.
58 Ibid.
59 Rule 22-1.a.
60 Rule 22-1.b. and 2.
61 Rule 14-4.
62 Rule 18-1.
63 Ibid.
64 Note 1 on rule 18.
65 Rule 18-5.
66 Rule 18-2.
67 Definition of "outside agency" in conj. with rule 13-1.
68 Rule 19-1.
69 Ibid.
70 Rule 19-1.b.
71 Rule 19-5.
72 Ibid.
73 Rule 19-2.b.
74 Definition of "outside agency" in conj. with rule 13-1.
75 Argumentum e contrario, rule 17-3.c. in conj. with rule 13-1.
76 Rule 17-3.
77 Rule 27-2.a.
78 Rule 27-1.
79 Rule 27-2.a.
80 Ibid.
81 Rule 27-2.a. in conj. with rule 27-1. and 20-5.
82 Rule 27-2.a.
83 Note on rule 27-2.a.
84 Rule 27-2.b.
85 Rule 27-2.c.
86 Note on rule 27-2.c.
87 Rule 27-2.b.
88 Ibid.
89 Decision 27/17.

5. On the tee

Punctuality. You should arrive at the 1ˢᵗ tee 10 minutes before your starting time and register with the starter (the person who is responsible for ensuring that the right people tee-off at the appropriate time). If you arrive after your starting time you are usually DISQUALIFIED[1]. You must ensure that you tee-off punctually.

Care. In order to protect the surface of the teeing ground, golf bags and golf trolleys should be placed adjacent to it and never on it.

Number of clubs. Check that you are carrying a *maximum of 14 clubs*. If you have brought too many you must remove the extra clubs from your bag *before beginning* the round[2]. If necessary, they are to be left at the tee.
If you only notice that you have too many clubs *after starting* the round you must immediately declare them to be out of play and you are then no longer permitted to use them, otherwise you will be disqualified[3].
You will incur 2 PENALTY STROKES for each hole on which you had too many clubs, to a maximum of 4 PENALTY STROKES per round[4].

Fellow-players. It is customary to greet your fellow-players and any caddies—the participants should also introduce themselves. You must remain in the group assigned for the entire round otherwise you will be disqualified[5].

Companions. If you would like to take somebody with you to accompany you on the round (who is not going to take on the role of a caddie) you should first inquire as to whether your fellow-competitors are in agreement. You should ensure that the accompanying person is familiar with the basic principles of the etiquette.

Local Rules. Make sure that you and your fellow-competitors are familiar with any special rules (local and temporary rules).

Score card. If you are playing in a competition check your score card once again and then swap it with a fellow-competitor (your marker). Remember to record your own score in the marker column of the other person's score card.

If you start on the 10th tee remember to record the result under hole no. 10 on the score card.

Score card. Swap your score card with a fellow-player if you are playing in a competition. Make sure that you note the scores in the correct place in the player's and the marker's column.

Player									Hcp			
Jeff Miller									19.8/24			

Competition	Audi Quattro Cup			Date	07.17.04
Stableford/ back tees					

Marker	Hole	Men champion	Men medal	Ladies champion	Ladies medal	Hcp	Par	Player			+0-
	1	380	345	335	315	7	4				
	2	370	350	315	295	9	4				
	3	490	475	445	420	15	5				
	4	175	160	155	140	11	3				
	5	325	275	270	235	17	4				
	6	560	520	495	460	3	5				

Order of play and honour. The order of play at the *first* tee is determined by the line up (list of tee times). If there is no list available the order is decided by drawing lots[6]. In friendly, non-competition rounds it has become customary to start in accordance with handicap, whereby the player with the lowest handicap has priority. The player who is entitled to tee-off first is said to have the "honour".

On all the *following* tees the person who had the best result at the previous hole has the honour. If two players had the same result they tee-off in the same order as on the previous tee[7].

However if a group is made up of players who are not playing from the same teeing grounds (e.g. men and women) the afore-mentioned rule does not strictly apply as the player who is playing from further back normally tees-off first to save time. Therefore the principle of "ladies first" does not apply to the game of golf.

Never tee-up before the player who has the honour before you has teed-off. If you have teed-up too soon it is a matter of courtesy to remove the ball again even if it supposedly does not disturb the player teeing-off.

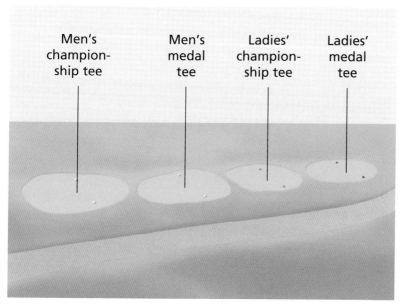

Men's
champion-
ship tee

Men's
medal
tee

Ladies'
champion-
ship tee

Ladies'
medal
tee

Tee positions. The men's tees are usually behind the ladies' tees whereas the championship tees are further from the hole than the medal tees. The tees are marked with different colours from country to country. White, yellow, black and red (from the back to the front) is a common colour scheme.

If a player tees-off out of turn, this is a breach of etiquette—but the stroke counts anyway and he does NOT INCUR A PENALTY[8]. However, if the players have agreed upon the wrong order so that one of them gains a tactical advantage they will be punished with DISQUALIFICATION[9].

Have a good game. It is customary to wish each other a good game before the first player tees-off.

Advice and line of play. You are free to talk about the overall length of the hole, about the location of hazards or out of bounds margins, about the rules and about other *matters of public information*[10]. However you are *not permitted* to *request or give advice* otherwise you will incur a 2 STROKE PENALTY[11]. (For example, the following questions and tips are not allowed: "Which club did you take?", "Which club should I play?", "If I was you I would use a 7 iron.", "Don't take such a big swing.")
If you cannot see the flag from the tee you are allowed to ask a fellow-player to describe the layout of the hole and to indicate the direction to the green. However caution is called for as tips on the best way to play the hole, on tactics or the ideal line would again be classed as advice[12].

Readiness. Ensure that you are prepared (have the club, tee, ball and spare ball ready) and that you always know when it is your turn.

Chipping and putting to kill time. If you have to wait on the tee because the group ahead of you is not yet out of reach you are allowed to practice a few putts and chips on or near the teeing ground to kill time[13]. (Please note that this is an exception and that taking practice shots is very restricted and is only allowed between holes.)

Teeing ground. The teeing ground extends from the two tee-markers to 2 club-lengths behind the markers[14]. The *ball* must be teed-up *within* this rectangular area, however a player can take up his stance outside it[15]. A ball is outside the teeing ground when the entire ball is outside it[16].

Teeing ground. The ball has to be teed-up within the teeing ground, whereas the player himself is allowed to take his stance outside this area. If a player has teed his ball up too far forward you should point this out to him—before he plays his stroke. This is a matter of courtesy and is not classed as advice.

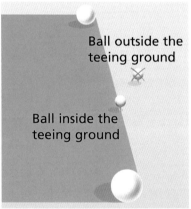

Ball outside the teeing ground

Ball inside the teeing ground

The tee-markers are classed as fixed objects *before the tee shot* and cannot be moved or repositioned before this shot has been taken—otherwise you will incur 2 PENALTY STROKES[17]. However after the stroke they are classed as movable obstructions and can be removed WITHOUT PENALTY[18]. (For example if you have mishit your stroke in such a way that the ball has come to rest behind a tee-marker you can then move this marker WITHOUT PENALTY and play the ball as it lies.)

If a player tees-off from outside the teeing ground the stroke it-self does not count and he incurs 2 PENALTY STROKES. The player has to rectify his mistake by teeing-off again within the teeing ground (3rd stroke)[19].

If the mistake is not rectified and the player continues to play his original ball he will be DISQUALIFIED[20]. (The same rule applies for playing from the *wrong* teeing ground[21], even if this is further back and the player therefore would not gain an advantage from it.)

Announcing the ball and teeing-up. Always inform your fellow-competitors of the brand and number of the ball, loudly and clearly. If two players are about to play the same ball it is advisable to swap one of them. It is particularly prudent to mark your own ball unambiguously with a personal symbol using a waterproof felt-tip pen—it can then be unmistakably identified as your own later.

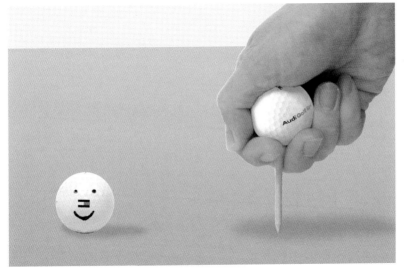

Marking the ball and teeing it up. It is advisable to mark the ball using a waterproof felt-tip pen.
The easiest way to tee-up is to put the tee into the ground with the ball already on it, rather than first pushing the tee into the ground and then trying to balance the ball on top of it.

Relief. On the teeing ground you are entitled to ideal starting conditions, therefore you are allowed to tee-up the ball[22], smooth out uneven ground[23] and even pull up grass[24]. All natural and artificial objects which interfere with play, such as leaves, grass, tees, cigarette ends etc. (but not including tee-markers), can be removed without penalty[25].

Practice swing. Please avoid taking practice swings on the teeing ground. If necessary, take practice swings next to the teeing ground as it is a confined area and needs particular care. Please do not take a practice swing in the direction of the group ahead of you if they are not yet out of reach—the players in front cannot tell from a distance whether you are hitting the ball or whether you are just taking a practice swing and this could put them off their game.

Concentration and courtesy. You should always remain absolutely silent when another player is addressing the ball or is playing a stroke (in particular do not move about or search around for things in your golf bag or trouser pockets). Ensure that your shadow does not disturb the player teeing-off. Out of courtesy and for safety reasons, please stand opposite the player on the teeing ground if possible.

Quiet, please. You should stand opposite a player and remain still and silent while he is concentrating on his shot. Rustling and jingling sounds would disturb his concentration.

Ball falls off tee. If the ball is accidentally knocked from the tee *before the first stroke*, i.e. the ball falls off the tee while not yet in play (e.g. when addressing the ball or because of an ill-fated practice swing), you will NOT INCUR A PENALTY and you can tee the ball up again[26]. (Despite the fact that other golfers may try to persuade you otherwise, this type of incident does not count as a stroke.)

Ball knocked off the tee. No need to worry—the ball can be teed up again and no penalty is incurred.

Air shot. If you miss the ball when you actually intended to hit it this stroke counts and the ball is in play[27] (i.e. you are no longer allowed to touch it).

Sighting the ball. Watch the ball you have hit (as well as those hit by your fellow-players) until it comes to *rest*. Make a mental note of any trees, bushes, stakes etc. close to the ball so that you can find it again straight away.

Tip. The easiest way to save as much as half an hour and five strokes on a round of golf is to keep your eye on the ball at all times. Use prominent features as a guide and always count the trees so that you know which tree to search next to. Experience has shown that the landscape looks totally different when you have finally reached the spot where you think the ball has landed.

Freeing up the teeing ground. Clear the teeing ground immediately and do not spend time looking for your tee if it has flown off. Please throw broken tees away in the container provided. On no account are tees to be embedded into the teeing ground, i.e. they are not to be rammed into the ground with the club.

Divots. Pieces of grass which have been hit out are not to be replaced on the teeing ground (any holes are to be filled in with the mixture of sand and grass seed which is usually provided).

Lost ball. If you are *absolutely sure* that your ball has landed out of bounds the ball is then classed as "lost". Wait until all the players have teed-off from the teeing ground in question and then bring a new ball into play under PENALTY OF 1 STROKE by announcing the new ball with brand and number, teeing it up somewhere within the teeing ground and playing your tee shot (3rd stroke)[29].

Provisional ball. If you only *suspect* that the ball has landed out of bounds, or that it could be impossible to find, you should play a provisional ball after all the players have teed-off from the teeing ground in question. Announce, loudly and clearly, that the ball being played is "provisional", stating the brand and number (it is advisable to use a different ball than the one you used for your first stroke). You are allowed to tee-up again[29]. Then play this ball until you reach the approximate position where you believe the original ball to be[30].

If you do not explicitly announce that the second ball is "provisional" it automatically becomes the new ball in play under PENALTY OF 1 STROKE. In this case, the original ball is "lost" and must not be played anymore under any circumstances[31]. This also applies if you have already looked for the ball for a while and only then return to the teeing ground. This is because a provisional ball is only classed as provisional if it is played *before* the player goes down the course to look for the first ball[32].

NB: The *process* of playing a provisional ball comes WITHOUT PENALTY. It also remains WITHOUT PENALTY if the original ball is found and is played again[33]. However if the provisional ball becomes the ball in play this, of course, incurs 1 PENALTY STROKE and all the strokes made count[34]—those with the original ball as well as those with the provisional ball.

Ball lands in a water hazard. If your ball has landed in a water hazard you do *not* have the option of playing a provisional ball[35]. This would also make no sense at all as you can proceed in accordance with the water hazard rule which is much more advantageous (see page 122ff.).

Ball lands on a different teeing ground. If your ball lands on a different teeing ground (e.g. on a teeing ground ahead of you) you are simply to continue to play the ball as it lies[36]. The tee-markers are then classed as movable obstructions and can be removed WITHOUT PENALTY[37].

Ball lands on the wrong fairway. If your ball lands on a neighbouring fairway this is not a great disaster as far as the rules are concerned because all fairways are part of "through the green". Play the ball as it lies[38], but in doing so make sure that you do not get in the way of those playing on this fairway—you do not have priority on the wrong fairway. (Please note—sometimes neighbouring fairways are designated out of bounds, in which case you would have to tee-off again incurring 1 PENALTY STROKE[39]. Look out for the appropriate markings.)

Wrong green. Even if your ball lands on the wrong green there is no need to tee-off again. The wrong green is also a part of "through the green" and you are given FREE RELIEF[40] (see page 103).

---

1 Rule 6-3.a.
2 Rule 4-4.a.
3 Rule 4-4.c.
4 Rule 4-4.
5 Rule 6-3.b.
6 Rule 10-2.a.
7 Ibid.
8 Rule 10-2.c
9 Ibid.
10 Definition of "advice".
11 Rule 8-1.
12 Definition of "advice".
13 Rule 7-2.
14 Definition of "teeing ground".
15 Rule 11-1.
16 Definition of "teeing ground".
17 Rule 11-2.
18 Rule 11-2. in conj. with rule 24-1.
19 Rule 11-4.b.
20 Ibid.
21 Rule 11-5.
22 Rule 11-1.
23 Rule 13-2.
24 Decision 13-2/3.
25 Rule 23 and rule 24.
26 Rule 11-3.
27 Definition of "stroke" in conj. with rule 11-3.
28 Rule 27-1. in conj. with rule 20-5.
29 Rule 27-2.a. in conj. with rule 27-1. and rule 20-5.
30 Rule 27-2.b.
31 Rule 27-2.a.
32 Ibid.
33 Rule 27-2.c.
34 Rule 27-2.b.
35 Rule 27-2.a. in conj. with exception 1 to rule 27-1.
36 Rule 13-1.
37 Rule 24-1. in conj. with rule 11-2.
38 Rule 13-1.
39 Rule 27-1. in conj. with rule 20-5.
40 Rule 25-3.

6. Through the green

Definition. The term "through the green" refers to the entire area of the course excluding the teeing ground and the green of the hole to be played, and excluding all the hazards and areas which are out of bounds[1]. In other words it includes every fairway and all areas of semi-rough, rough and fringe, plus all other teeing grounds, as well as greens which do *not belong* to the hole. If you are on any other part of the course (teeing ground, bunker, water hazard, out of bounds, green) please refer to the relevant chapter.

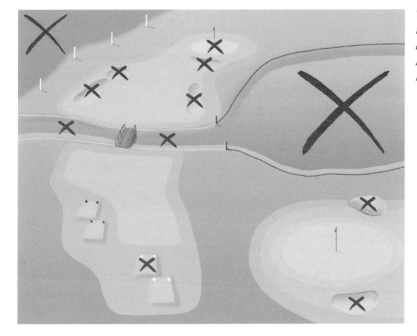

Through the green covers the largest area of the golf course—everything illustrated apart from the areas which have been crossed out.

Order of play. It is always the turn of the player whose ball is the farthest away from the hole[2]. Not keeping to the correct order of play does NOT INCUR A PENALTY as long as no agreement has been made with the intention of giving one of the players a tactical advantage[3]. However it can be a breach of etiquette.

Balls close to each other. If two balls are so close together that they obstruct each other, one ball can be marked and picked up until the other one has been played[4]. The ball is then to be put back precisely in its original position. If the original lie has been changed due to the other ball being played, you are to place your ball in the nearest position which is as similar as possible to the original lie—but of course, not nearer to the hole[5].

Looking for a ball. If you cannot find the ball straight away and have to start looking for it you should get into the habit of checking your watch. After a search time of 5 minutes the ball is classed as lost and is not to be played any more under any circumstances[6] (see page 105, "lost ball"). You should take a quick look behind before starting the search and let a group through if there is one waiting. In order to avoid misunderstandings you should inform your fellow-competitors of the brand and number of the missing ball once again before you start looking for it.

Tip. If you find your ball in the rough and have to return to your golf bag to fetch a club you should leave your cap, glove or another object by the ball to ensure that you can find the spot again.

Ball moved during a search. If you unintentionally move the ball during the search you must put it back and you will receive 1 PENALTY STROKE[7]. However if a fellow-competitor is responsible for the ball being moved this comes WITHOUT PENALTY for both players and the ball must again be put back[8]. If you do not put it back you will be playing from the wrong spot and you will incur 2 PENALTY STROKES[9].

Identifying the ball. If you cannot tell whether the ball found is yours you can mark its position and pick it up to identify it. However, before doing so you must inform your marker or a fellow-player of this and give him the opportunity to observe the entire procedure, otherwise you will incur 1 PENALTY STROKE[10]. If the ball is dirty you are permitted to scrape off the amount of dirt needed to identify it. The ball must then be put back in exactly the same position.

In order to avoid being suspected of trying to improve the lie you can ask a fellow-competitor to identify the ball for you. However caution is called for—some players think that they are behaving within the realms of "fair play" when they put your ball back in a slightly better position after identifying it or flatten the grass down around your ball in doing so. Such behaviour would result in 2 PENALTY STROKES for the other player[11] and this would also apply to you too if you were to go along with an improvement of this kind[12].

Advice and line of play. You are permitted to inquire about margins to areas which are out of bounds, pin positions and the position of hazards, or about other *matters of public information,* such as the rules[13]. You are also allowed to ask about the distance from *fixed* objects (for example distance markers, bunkers or a nearby tree) to the green. However you are *not permitted* to inquire about the distance from your ball to the green as this would be advice[14]. If you *request for* or *give* advice a 2 STROKE PENALTY will be incurred[15].

If you cannot see the flag or the green you are allowed to ask a fellow-player to indicate the line of play. However the other player is not permitted to remain on the line of play while you are making your stroke[16].

Playing the ball as it lies. Always bear in mind that the principle of the game of golf states that a ball must be played as it lies if the rules do not make provisions to the contrary[17]. You have to accept the lie as you find it. In particular, never attempt to improve the lie of the ball, the area of the intended stance or swing or the line of play in an unauthorised manner. You are not permitted to *move, bend or break off* anything growing or fixed *before* making a stroke. When addressing the ball you are only to ground the club gently and not press it into the ground. Breaches of this rule are punished with 2 PENALTY STROKES[18].

Play the ball as it lies.
Unjustified improvement of the ball's lie, the line of play or the area of stance or swing is penalised with 2 penalty strokes.

The only exception is when *taking up your stance,* when it is possible that moving, bending or breaking off something is *unavoidable.* This does NOT INCUR A PENALTY if it occurs when taking one's stance *fairly,* i.e. the player is not trying to gain an unjustified advantage but, for example, accidentally snaps off a small branch when entering a copse[19].

Practice swing. Practice swings are generally permitted through the green but please do not make practice swings while a fellow-competitor is playing his shot as this could disturb his concentration. It is advisable to take practice swings from a spot far enough away from the ball to avoid the risk of moving the ball unintentionally. Avoid damaging the grass when making practice swings if at all possible. Always replace any divots made and tread them in well or fill them in with sand.

If you rip something off, bend or break something when making your practice swing, thus creating an advantage for the ensuing shot, you will incur 2 PENALTY STROKES[23].

Ball moved when taking a practice swing. If you take a practice swing and accidentally move your ball in doing so this does not count as a stroke (as you did not intend to hit the ball[24]) and you are to put the ball back with 1 PENALTY STROKE[25]. If you do *not* put it back you will incur 2 PENALTY STROKES for playing from the wrong spot[26].

Ball moved when addressing the ball. If your ball moves after you have addressed it (i.e. after taking your stance and grounding

Tip. If the ball has an awkward or unsteady lie (e.g. on a slope, on leaves, in long grass or in a strong wind) it is advisable not to ground the club, as the ball might move.

your club[20]) it will be classed as having been moved by you and you must put it back, under PENALTY OF 1 STROKE[21]. If you do not put it back you will be playing from the wrong spot and you will therefore incur 2 PENALTY STROKES[22].

Loose impediments. Loose impediments are all *natural* objects which are *loose,* i.e. not fixed, not growing, nor firmly embedded or sticking to the ball (therefore this term does not include foliage growing on a tree, a branch which is dead but which is still fixed to the tree, creepers and climbing plants and an embedded stone etc.). Sand and loose soil are only classed as loose impediments on the green[27].

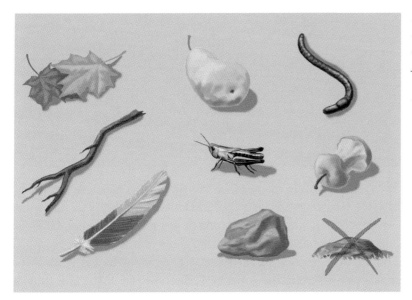

You are permitted to remove loose impediments WITHOUT PENALTY anywhere through the green[28]. However if your ball moves in doing so you must put it back under PENALTY OF 1 STROKE[29]. If you do not put it back you will incur 2 PENALTY STROKES for playing from the wrong spot[30].

If you suspect that your ball could be moved when you remove loose impediments it is advisable to play it as it lies instead of taking any unnecessary risks.

Obstructions. *Artificial* (man-made) objects are termed obstructions. They are divided into *movable* and *immovable* obstructions. However, no objects which are used to define out of bounds are classed as obstructions[31].

Movable obstructions. Movable obstructions include all artificial objects which can be *moved* with a reasonable amount of effort and within an appropriate length of time (except for out of bounds posts)[32].

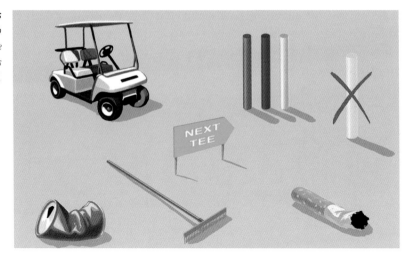

You are permitted to remove movable obstructions anywhere WITHOUT PENALTY. If your ball moves on doing so you must put it back WITHOUT PENALTY[33]. If you do not put it back you will incur 2 PENALTY STROKES for playing from the wrong spot[34].

You are also entitled to FREE RELIEF even if the ball is lying *in* or *on* the movable obstruction. Mark the position of the ball underneath the obstruction. Then pick the ball up, remove the obstruction and *drop* the ball as near as possible to the position marked[35].

Immovable obstructions. Immovable obstructions are artificial objects which *cannot be moved* (except for posts, fences, walls etc. which delineate out of bounds)[36].

You are only given relief WITHOUT PENALTY from an immovable obstruction if it interferes with your *stance* or your *swing* (interference with the line of play is not sufficient)[37].

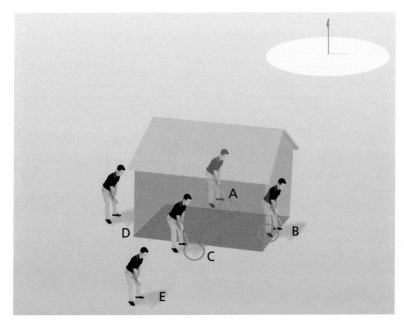

Interference *by an immovable obstruction only occurs when the player's stance or swing is physically obstructed. In the illustration with the hut this is the case with points A (backswing), B (stance) and C (follow through) and the player is entitled to free relief. In the case of D and E the player can take his stance freely and make a swing without interference, therefore the ball has to be played as it lies. Whether or not the hut is in his line of play is immaterial.*

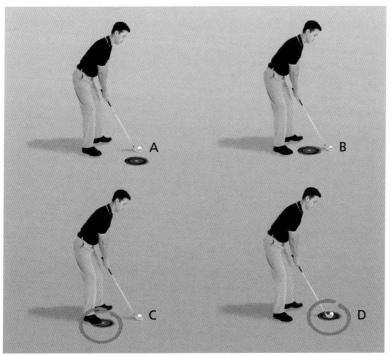

No interference. *An immovable obstruction does not cause an interference if the player is only obstructed visually or feels impeded in any other way. In the illustration with the sprinkler head this is the case with points A and B and the player is not entitled to free relief. However, in the case of C and D the player cannot take up his stance freely or make his swing without interference and he is therefore given free relief.*

To take relief WITHOUT PENALTY from immovable obstructions proceed as follows: First, determine the spot through the green which is nearest to the ball and where you are no longer obstructed. This point is not to be closer to the hole. Then drop the ball within 1 club-length[38].

A cart path is an immovable obstruction (artificial) and the player is entitled to free relief if his ball is on the road (swing is obstructed) or if he would have to stand on the path (stance obstructed). Determine the nearest spot where you can take your stance and make your swing without obstruction and take a drop within 1 club-length.

However you do *not have to* take relief. In some cases it might be prudent to play the ball as it lies, especially when the nearest point of relief is behind a tree, in the rough or in an unfavourable position of any kind (nearest point, not nicest point of relief!).

Caution. You cannot choose which side of the cart path to drop on. It must be the side where the nearest point is. In the illustration the player has to go to the left, to point A. While point B is the same distance away it is not far enough as the player has to take complete relief and is not permitted to take up his stance on the path. Point C is further away than point A. (The situation would be reversed if the player was left-handed.)

Please note that some Local Rules declare certain facilities (e.g. roads and paths) to be an integral part of the course therefore relief WITHOUT PENALTY IS NOT given in these cases[39].

Abnormal ground conditions. *Casual water* (sites where water has temporarily collected e.g. puddles, ice and snow)[40] as well as *ground under repair* (GUR, usually marked with blue stakes, lines etc. or mentioned in the Local Rules)[41] are classed as abnormal ground conditions. The term also includes certain precisely defined animal tracks such as *holes, casts or paths* of *burrowing animals, reptiles and birds*[42].

Abnormal ground conditions. This mainly includes two particular conditions—puddles and ground under repair (usually marked in blue).
Although the tracks of certain types of animals are also included, in practice they rarely play an important role. Animals do not usually wait next to their tracks and this makes them difficult to identify.

If you move your ball unintentionally when searching in abnormal ground conditions the ball must be put back and in this particular case you do NOT INCUR A PENALTY[43].

If your ball is *lying in* abnormal ground conditions or your *stance* or *swing* is obstructed by abnormal ground conditions you can take relief WITHOUT PENALTY by determining the nearest point through the green where the condition no longer causes interference and drop the ball within 1 club-length[44] (the same procedure as for immovable obstructions). In doing so you must bear in mind that, as always, this spot cannot be closer to the hole than the ball's original position.

In this case too you do not have to take relief and are permitted to play the ball as it lies (as long as the Local Rules do not specify that taking relief is compulsory e.g. in order to protect young plants).

Through the green

Ground under repair is usually marked in blue or mentioned in the Local Rules. Find the nearest point where the ball is no longer in GUR and where you do not have to take your stance within it and drop the ball within 1 club-length, without penalty.

Ball lost in abnormal ground conditions. If you are absolutely positive that your ball can only be lost in abnormal ground conditions and not anywhere else you will also be given FREE RELIEF (however, if you only *suspect* this to be the case it is to be treated as an ordinary "lost ball", see page 105). First of all determine the point where the ball last entered the area concerned. From this point you determine the nearest point of relief through the green, not closer to the hole, and drop a new ball WITHOUT PENALTY within 1 club-length[45].

Ball lost in abnormal ground conditions. The same procedure as above, however in this case the starting point is not the ball, but the point where the ball last crossed the margin of the GUR.

Wrong green. If your *ball* lands on the wrong green you are *not* permitted to play it from there as in doing so the green could be damaged. You *have to* take relief WITHOUT PENALTY in a similar way to the procedure described under abnormal ground conditions. Determine the nearest point, not closer to the hole, which is neither on the green nor in a hazard and drop the ball within 1 club-length[46].

Wrong green. In order to protect the green, playing from the wrong green is never permitted. The ball has to be dropped within 1 club-length of the nearest point of relief, without penalty. NB: This point is always on the fringe. The player is permitted to stand on the wrong green to play a ball which is not on this green.

Embedded ball. If the ball is embedded in its *own* pitch-mark on any *closely-mown* area (fairway, fringe) it can be picked up, cleaned and dropped WITHOUT PENALTY right next to the spot where it was lying, not closer to the hole[47].

Ball in its own pitch mark. *Relief is given from an embedded ball through the green (but not in hazards), however only if the ball has become embedded in a closely-mown area (i.e. the fairway, fringe— not the semi-rough or the rough!).*

Divots, tractor ruts, bald or dry patches etc. If your ball ends up in a bad position which is not explicitly dealt with by the rules (nor by the Local Rules) then there is nothing you can do about it. You have to play the ball as it lies[48] unless you declare it unplayable, accepting 1 PENALTY STROKE (see following page).

Ball in a divot. *Put it down to experience—bad lies are part of the game. The ball has to be played as it lies. It could, of course, be declared unplayable but this would mean 1 penalty stroke.*

Unplayable ball. You can declare your ball unplayable through the green *at any time*. Whether the ball, objectively speaking, actually is unplayable or not is irrelevant. Declaring one's ball to be unplayable is a free decision which any player can make and it does not need to be agreed upon with the marker. You then have the following options[49]:

1. Under PENALTY OF 1 STROKE, drop a ball within 2 club-lengths, not closer to the hole. (Please note—the starting point for measuring the 2 club-lengths is the ball's *original* position, *not* the next "playable" spot!)
2. Under PENALTY OF 1 STROKE, drop the ball on the backwards extension of the line from the hole to the ball at any distance wished.
3. Under PENALTY OF 1 STROKE, drop the ball as near as possible to the spot where the last stroke was made. If this was at the tee the ball can be teed-up again.

__Unplayable ball.__ 3 options are available for dropping if a ball is declared unplayable, each of which incurs 1 penalty stroke.

Unplayable lie.
If the ball is in a hopeless position it is advisable to accept 1 penalty stroke and to declare the ball unplayable.

Lost ball. If you do not find the ball within 5 minutes it is classed as lost[50] and you have no other choice than to bring another ball into play under PENALTY OF 1 STROKE. Announce the new ball again with the brand and number and drop it as near as possible to the place where you made your last stroke. If you took your last stroke from the tee you are also permitted to tee-up the new ball[51].

However if you have already played a provisional ball you do not need to return to this spot and the provisional ball becomes the ball in play under PENALTY OF 1 STROKE[52].

Balls through the green which cannot be conclusively identified as your own[53], as well as balls which are out of bounds[35] are also classed as lost[54].

Lost ball. *If a ball is lost the player only has one option—to return to the position of the last stroke and to drop a new ball under penalty of 1 stroke (penalty of stroke and distance). If this spot was on the tee, the player can tee the new ball up again.*

Wrong ball. If you suddenly realise that you have been playing with the wrong ball you are to rectify the mistake by returning and playing the *correct* ball (the wrong ball should be put back). The strokes which you have made with the wrong ball do not count, however you will be given 2 PENALTY STROKES for the initial mistake[55].

Wrong ball. Playing the wrong ball is irritating as it costs the player 2 penalty strokes. However at least the strokes played with the wrong ball do not count. The player is not to continue playing with the wrong ball under any circumstances—this would mean disqualification.

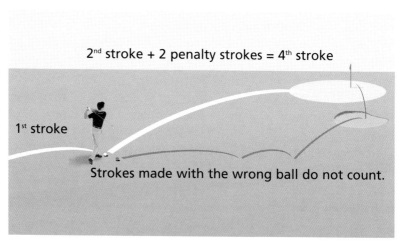

2nd stroke + 2 penalty strokes = 4th stroke

1st stroke

Strokes made with the wrong ball do not count.

However, if you do not find the correct ball again it is classed as lost in accordance with the rules. You must return to the position where you *last* played a stroke with the *correct* ball and drop a new ball under PENALTY OF 1 ADDITIONAL STROKE[56].

If you hole-out with the wrong ball and do not rectify the mistake immediately afterwards you will be DISQUALIFIED[57].

Therefore it is advisable to get into the habit of taking a close look at the ball to make sure that it is actually yours before playing each stroke.

Ball hits an outside agency/ rub of the green. If your ball hits an electricity pole, a tree, a spectator, an animal or any other "outside agency" you do NOT INCUR A PENALTY and the ball has to be played as it lies[58].

Ball hits another ball. If your ball hits another ball NO PENALTY is incurred and you have to play your ball as it lies. The ball which was moved is to be put back[59].

(NB: 2 PENALTY STROKES are incurred on the green only—if both balls were at rest on the green before the shot was made[60], see page 144.)

Ball hits the player himself or his equipment. If you yourself or your equipment (golf bag, electric cart etc.) are hit by your ball 2 PENALTY STROKES will be incurred and the ball has to be played as it lies[61] (the piece of equipment concerned can be removed before the next stroke).

Ball at rest moved by an outside agency. If your ball at rest is moved by an outside agency (e.g. spectator, animal, fellow-competitor, other ball) you have to put your ball back WITHOUT PENALTY. If your ball has been picked up and taken away you are permitted to place a new ball on the spot where the original ball was lying, WITHOUT PENALTY[62]. However, if your ball has disappeared without you seeing whether an outside agency has taken it or not, the ball is to be treated as an ordinary "lost ball" (see page 105).

Striking the ball more than once. If you accidentally strike the ball more than once when playing a shot (e.g. because the club gets caught up in the rough) you have to add 1 PENALTY STROKE to it[63].

Striking the ball twice. Sometimes the club gets caught up in the rough, thereby striking the ball twice. If this happens the stroke counts, plus 1 penalty stroke.

Ball lands on a different teeing ground or on a wrong fairway.
If your ball lands on a different teeing ground or on a neighbouring fairway this is not a great disaster as far as the rules are
concerned. Both of these are part of "through the green" and the
ball has to be played as it lies[64] (after the tee shot has been played
the tee-markers are classed as movable obstructions and can be
removed WITHOUT PENALTY[65]).

1 Definition of "through the green" in conj. with definition of "course".
2 Rule 10-2.b.
3 Rule 10-2.c.
4 Rule 22.
5 Rule 20-3.b.(i).
6 Definition of "lost ball".
7 Rule 18-2.
8 Rule 18-1.
9 Rule 20-6.b. in conj. with rule 18.
10 Rule 12-2.
11 Rule 1-2.
12 Rule 13-2.
13 Definition of "advice".
14 Decision 8-1/2.
15 Rule 8-1.
16 Rule 8-2.a.
17 Rule 13-1.
18 Rule 13-2.
19 Ibid.
20 Definition of "addressing the ball".
21 Rule 18-2.b.
22 Rule 20-6.b. in conj. with rule 18.
23 Rule 13-2.
24 Definition of "stroke".
25 Rule 18-2.a.
26 Rule 20-6.b. in conj. with rule 18.
27 Definition of "loose impediments".
28 Rule 23-1.
29 Rule 18-2.c.
30 Rule 20-6.b. in conj. with rule 18.
31 Definition of "obstructions".
32 Ibid.
33 Rule 24.1.a.
34 Rule 20-6.b. in conj. with rule 24.
35 Rule 24-1.b.
36 Definition of "obstructions".
37 Rule 24-2.a.
38 Rule 24-2.b.
39 Definition of "obstructions".
40 Definition of "casual water".
41 Definition of "ground under repair".
42 Definition of "abnormal ground conditions".
43 Rule 12-1.
44 Rule 25-1.a. and b.
45 Rule 25-1.c.
46 Rule 25-3.
47 Rule 25-2.
48 Rule 13-1.
49 Rule 28.
50 Definition of "lost ball".
51 Rule 27-1. in conj. with rule 20-5.
52 Rule 27-2.b.
53 Definition of "lost ball".
54 Rule 27-1.
55 Rule 15-3.
56 Rule 27-1.
57 Rule 15-3.
58 Rule 19-1.
59 Rule 19-5.
60 Rule 19-5. in conj. with rule 16-1.f.
61 Rule 19-2.b.
62 Rule 18-1. and 5.
63 Rule 14-4.
64 Rule 13-1.
65 Rule 24-1. in conj. with rule 11-2.

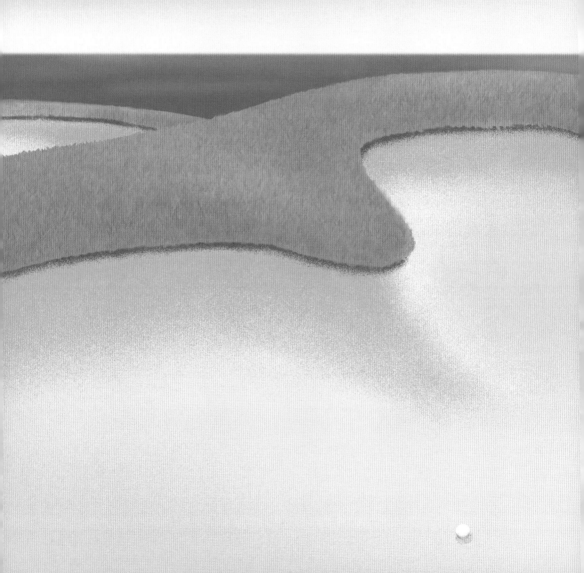

7. In the bunker

Definition. The margin of the bunker is formed by the natural edge of the sand. Areas of grass inside the bunker are not classed as being part of it and sand sprayed over the bunker edge is also no longer a part of the bunker. A ball is classed as being in a bunker if it touches the sand within it[1].

NB: Sand sprayed over the edge of the bunker can only be removed on the green.

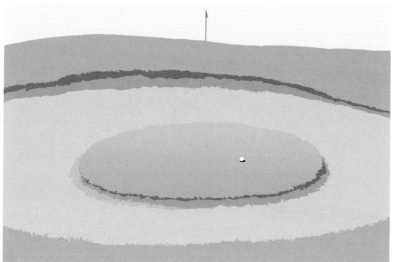

Areas of grass in the bunker are not, according to the rules, a part of the bunker but are classed as "through the green", i.e. you are permitted to ground the club on areas of grass in the bunker and you are also permitted to remove loose impediments (except for sand).

Care and saving time. On entering a bunker please ensure that you do so from the shallow side and not over the steep bunker wall. Always take the shortest route and take the rake in with you if possible. However in a bunker you are only allowed to drop the rake or to put it down, but you are not permitted to push it into the sand, as this would be classed as testing the sand, which is not allowed[2].

Balls close to each other. If two balls are so close together that they obstruct each other, one ball can be marked and picked up until the other one has been played[3].

The ball is then to be put back precisely in its original position. If the original lie of the ball has been changed in playing the other ball it must be recreated as accurately as possible, i.e. if appropriate, rake the sand, bury the ball etc.[4].

No identification and wrong ball. In a hazard you are *not* permitted to pick up the ball to identify it[5]. If you cannot tell whether the ball found is your own, but you suspect that this is the case, play the ball as if it were your own. Then, before playing your first stroke outside the hazard it is imperative that you first check whether it actually was your ball. If you discover that you have been playing with the wrong ball you are to remedy the mistake by returning and playing the correct ball (the wrong ball should be put back). The strokes made with the wrong ball do not count and you do NOT INCUR ANY PENALTY STROKES for playing the wrong ball *from a hazard*[6].

Advice and line of play. You are allowed to ask about the pin position, the position of other hazards, out of bounds margins and other matters of public information (e.g. the rules or Local Rules)[7]. You are also permitted to inquire about the distance from a fixed object (distance marker, edge of the bunker etc.) to the green. However you are not allowed to ask about the distance from your ball to the green or questions on how to play a shot as this would be advice[8]. 2 PENALTY STROKES are incurred in the event that advice is asked for or given[9].

If you cannot see the flag from your position in the bunker you are allowed to ask a fellow-player to indicate the line of play. However the other player must leave this line before you make your stroke[10].

Playing the ball as it lies. You are not permitted to test the condition of the sand before playing your stroke and therefore you are also not allowed to touch the sand. In particular you are not permitted to ground the club in the sand before making a stroke nor to touch the sand on your backswing. A breach of this rule incurs 2 PENALTY STROKES[11].

However you are allowed to put down the rake in the bunker as long as you do not test the sand in doing so[12]. This also applies if you take more than one club into the bunker and you put those which you are not going to use down while playing your shot.

Naturally, you are not permitted to smooth out any tracks in the bunker before making your stroke. If your ball lands in footprints made by a previous player you must play the ball as it lies, however annoying this may be. It is therefore of utmost importance to rake the bunker and to leave it in perfect condition.

No contact with the sand.
The sand in the bunker is not to be touched before the stroke is played (2 penalty strokes). Therefore the club is not to be grounded but must be held slightly above the sand when the ball is being addressed. Caution is even required with the backswing as touching the sand is also forbidden in this case too.

Practice swing. In principle you are also allowed to take practice swings in the bunker, however in doing so you are not permitted to touch the sand[13]. It might therefore be advisable to make a few practice swings outside the bunker before entering it.

Ball moved when addressing the ball. If your ball moves after you have addressed it (i.e. after taking your stance without grounding your club[14]), it is classed as being moved by you and you must put it back, under PENALTY OF 1 STROKE[15]. If you do not put it back you will be playing from the wrong spot and you will therefore incur 2 PENALTY STROKES[16].

Loose impediments. Loose impediments, such as twigs, leaves, stones* etc. must not be removed or touched in a bunker otherwise you will incur 2 PENALTY STROKES[17].
* Bear the Local Rules in mind—they often stipulate that stones in bunkers are classed as movable obstructions and may therefore be removed WITHOUT PENALTY by way of exception.

Obstructions. Movable obstructions, e.g. the rake, can be removed from the bunker WITHOUT PENALTY, as described above (Through the green, see page 98)[18]. If the sand is touched in doing so this is also WITHOUT PENALTY[19]. If the ball moves while the obstruction is being removed the ball is to be put back WITHOUT PENALTY[20]. If the ball does not stay in position after it has been put back it is to be put back once more. If this happens a second time the ball is to be placed at the nearest point in the bunker, not nearer to the hole, where the ball does not move[21].

In the bunker

Loose impediments and movable obstructions.
While loose impediments (natural) are not to be removed in a bunker, movable obstructions (artificial) can be removed. Stones are, by definition, loose impediments but the Local Rules often class them as movable obstructions if they are in a bunker, in which case they can be removed without penalty.

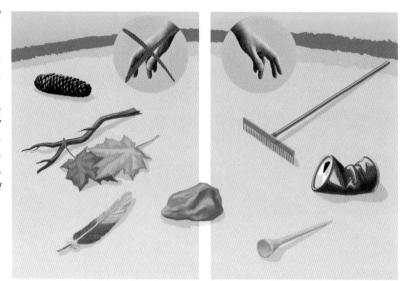

The rake *is a movable obstruction and can therefore be removed without penalty—even if the ball comes to rest directly on the rake. If the ball moves when taking the rake away it is to be put back without penalty.*

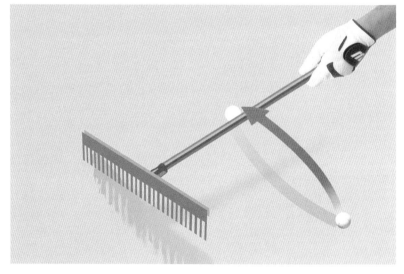

FREE RELIEF is also given from immovable obstructions in the bunker if they interfere with the player's stance or swing[22]—however immovable obstructions are hardly ever found in bunkers (in rare cases steps and supporting walls are built into the sides of bunkers). The procedure would be the same as through the green (see page 100), whereby the ball would, of course, have to be dropped *within the bunker,* WITHOUT PENALTY. Another possibility would be to drop the ball *outside* the bunker, then incurring 1 PENALTY STROKE, in accordance with the procedure for abnormal ground conditions in the bunker—see below.

Abnormal ground conditions. If the ball is lying in abnormal ground conditions in a bunker (casual water, GUR, certain animal tracks) or if these interfere with your stance or swing you can take FREE RELIEF and use one of the following options:

1. WITHOUT PENALTY, drop the ball *in the bunker*, at the nearest point, not closer to the hole, where interference from the condition is eliminated to the largest possible extent, within 1 club-length[23].
2. WITH 1 PENALTY STROKE, drop the ball *outside the bunker* on the backwards extension of the line from the hole to the ball[24].

Puddles in the bunker.
The player is also entitled to free relief in a bunker if abnormal ground conditions interfere with his stance or swing. However he always has to drop the ball inside the bunker and not nearer to the flag.
As it is possible that an appropriate spot cannot be found another option is available outside the bunker—however this involves 1 penalty stroke.

If the bunker is completely flooded the player has no other choice than to proceed in accordance with the 2nd option. He then has to accept 1 PENALTY STROKE.

In the bunker

Buried lie, old footprints, interference from the edge of the bunker etc. The player faces a particular challenge if his ball has become buried in the sand (this lie is sometimes called a "fried egg"). This also applies to a ball which has landed in the footprints of a previous player or to a ball which is so near to the edge of the bunker that it is practically impossible to play. These lies are a part of the game and the ball has to be played as it lies[25]— unless you declare it unplayable (with 1 PENALTY STROKE, see below).

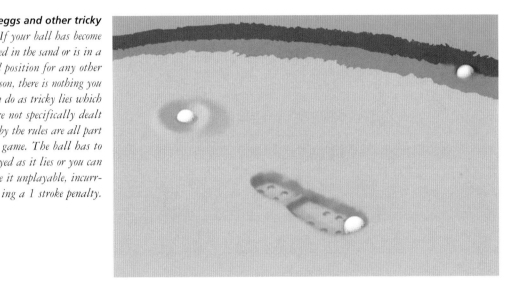

Fried eggs and other tricky lies. If your ball has become buried in the sand or is in a bad position for any other reason, there is nothing you can do as tricky lies which are not specifically dealt with by the rules are all part of the game. The ball has to be played as it lies or you can declare it unplayable, incurring a 1 stroke penalty.

Unplayable ball. You can declare your ball unplayable in a bunker at any time and use one of the following options[26]:

1. To take a drop *in the bunker* within 2 club-lengths, not closer to the hole, under PENALTY OF 1 STROKE.
2. To take a drop *in the bunker* on the backwards extension of the line from the hole to the ball under PENALTY OF 1 STROKE.
3. To take a drop as near as possible to the spot where the last stroke was played under PENALTY OF 1 STROKE. If this was at the tee the ball can be teed-up again. (This does not refer to the place where the last stroke was played outside the bunker, but to the position of the last actual stroke. This position can be inside or outside the bunker, depending on where the last stroke was taken from.)

Unplayable ball in a bunker. A ball can also be declared unplayable in a bunker and there are again three options available for dropping a ball—each of which incurs 1 penalty stroke. It must be borne in mind however that a ball in a bunker which is declared unplayable must usually be dropped in the bunker again. Exception: If the last stroke was played from outside the bunker the ball can also be dropped outside the bunker under penalty of stroke and distance.

Ball hits outside agency/ rub of the green. If your ball hits the rake or any other "outside agency" this is deemed a rub of the green, you do NOT INCUR A PENALTY and you have to continue playing the ball as it lies[27].

Ball hits the player himself or his equipment. If you yourself or your equipment (golf bag, electric cart etc.) are hit by your ball 2 PENALTY STROKES will be incurred and the ball has to be played as it lies[28].

Ball comes to rest in the bunker again. If, after the stroke, your ball rolls back into your own prints in the sand there is nothing you can do about it. You have to play the ball as it lies[29] or you can declare it unplayable (with 1 PENALTY STROKE, see above).
If you have hit the ball so that it is lying further in front of the same bunker, you are allowed to rake your marks before you play your next shot but you are still not permitted to touch the sand with your club (i.e. you are not to touch the sand when making a practice swing)[30].

117

Ball hit out of bounds/ lost ball. If you have hit your ball from the bunker out of bounds or to a place where you cannot find it, it is classed as lost in accordance with the rules. You have to drop a new ball on the spot where the last stroke was played from, with 1 PENALTY STROKE[31]—back into the bunker in this case. However you are then allowed to rake the sand before dropping the ball[32].

Striking the ball more than once. If you accidentally strike the ball more than once when playing a shot you have to add 1 PENALTY STROKE to it[33].

Raking. When raking, please take the time to ensure that you have smoothed out your marks in the sand meticulously—after all, no golfer likes having to hit their ball from hastily raked sand dunes or even from footprints made by a previous player. If there is no rake available you can smooth out your marks with a club if needs be.

Also, please observe the golf club's directives on where to place the rake. On some courses rakes are to be put down in the bunker, on others they are to be placed outside the bunker, whereas some clubs stipulate that rakes are to be carried on the golf cart. If the rake is to be put down in the bunker the best place to position it is at an angle of 90° to the edge of the bunker. On no account should the rake simply be thrown into the middle of the bunker.

Placing the rake. If the rake is put down in the bunker, it should be placed so that the handle is on the edge of the bunker to make it easy to pick it up. It is also best to position the rake at an angle of 90° to the bunker's edge so that balls do not get stuck near to the edge of the bunker but can roll into the flatter section.

1 Definition of "bunker".

2 Decision 13-4/22.

3 Rule 22.

4 Rule 20-3.b.

5 Rule 12-2.

6 Rule 15-3.

7 Definition of "advice".

8 Decision 8-1/2.

9 Rule 8-1.

10 Rule 8-2.a.

11 Rule 13-4.a. and b.

12 Decision 13-4/20.

13 Rule 13-4.b.

14 Definition of "addressing the ball".

15 Rule 18-2.b.

16 Rule 20-7.c. in conj. with rule 18.

17 Rule 13-4.c. and 23.1.

18 Rule 24-1.

19 Exception 1.a. to rule 13-4.

20 Rule 24-1.

21 Rule 20-3.d.(II).

22 Rule 24-2.

23 Rule 25-1.b.

24 Ibid.

25 Rule 13-1.

26 Rule 28.

27 Rule 19-1.

28 Rule 19-2.b.

29 Rule 13-1.

30 Exception 2. to rule 13-4.

31 Rule 27-1.

32 Rule 20-5. in conj. with exception 2. to rule 13-4. Also see decision 13-4/37.

33 Rule 14-4.

8. In a water hazard

Markings. Regular water hazards are marked with yellow stakes or lines, whereas lateral water hazards are marked with red stakes or lines[1].

Margin. Only the lines, or if there are stakes their connection in a straight line, are decisive in defining the margin of a water hazard (lines have priority over stakes). Whether or not there is actually any water within this margin is not important; the differentiation between wet and dry is therefore not a valid criteria.

A single water course can include both a regular water hazard and a lateral water hazard if they merge into each other.

A ball is in a water hazard as soon as it touches its margin (it does not have to lie completely within it). The stakes themselves are within the hazard, i.e. the margin runs along the outside of them[2].

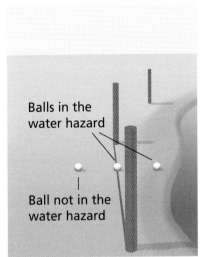

Balls in the water hazard

Ball not in the water hazard

Margin of a water hazard.
The ball is in the water hazard if it touches its margin.
NB: The official rules do not use the term "regular" but only differentiate between water hazards and lateral water hazards. However the term is used throughout this book as it makes it easier to distinguish between the two types of water hazard.

Caution. On entering a water hazard please ensure that you do not damage the embankment and disturb any nesting birds. You should leave your golf trolley and bag outside the hazard. Environmentally-sensitive areas should not be entered under any circumstances.

Please be careful as the ground in and around water hazards is often slippery. Furthermore, in some areas alligators could represent a real danger.

Ball only thought to be in the water hazard. If your ball has merely flown in the *direction* of the water hazard and has disappeared but you are not sure whether it actually did land in the hazard it is to be treated as an ordinary "lost ball", i.e. one lost outside a water hazard. You have to return to the position where you played your last stroke from and bring a new ball into play by taking a drop (tee-up on the teeing ground) under PENALTY OF 1 STROKE[3].

In a water hazard

Ball in a water hazard—options. If your ball is in a water hazard, i.e. you can see it in the hazard or it has disappeared but you have a legitimate reason to assume that it could only have come to rest within the water hazard and not anywhere else, you basically have two options:

1. **WITHOUT PENALTY, play the ball from the water hazard as it lies.** You simply play the ball from the hazard as it lies—under consideration of certain points (see page 125)[4].

2. **With 1 PENALTY STROKE, take a drop outside the water hazard.** You proceed in accordance with the water hazard rule and take a drop outside the hazard under PENALTY OF 1 STROKE (see below)[5].

Playing the ball as it lies.
This option comes into consideration if the ball has been found and is lying near the bank or if the water hazard is completely dried out. However please remember that if the water hazard in question is an environmentally-sensitive area which cannot be entered, this option does not apply and you have to take a drop under penalty of 1 stroke.

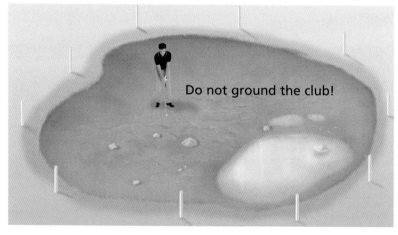

Do not ground the club!

Water hazard rule. Proceeding in accordance with the water hazard rule comes into consideration if the ball has a bad lie in the water hazard, if it has been lost in the hazard or if you are simply not permitted to play it from there.

Water hazard rule. In most cases the ball is immersed in the water and the player has no other choice than to proceed in accordance with the water hazard rule, thereby accepting 1 PENALTY STROKE. However even if the ball has been found in the water hazard, the tricky conditions and the risk which a shot would involve mean that it is often advisable to take a drop in accordance with the water hazard rule anyway. You then have the following options:

1. To take a drop at any desired distance on the backwards extension of the line from the hole to the entry point (point X where the ball last crossed the margin of the water hazard) under PENALTY OF 1 STROKE[6].
2. To take a drop as near as possible to the spot where the last stroke was played from under PENALTY OF 1 STROKE. If this was at the tee the new ball can be teed-up[7].

Regular water hazard.
Generally speaking, you are always permitted to play a ball in a water hazard as it lies. In addition, in the case of a regular water hazard (yellow) the player has two dropping options outside of the hazard—each of these options involves 1 penalty stroke.

If the ball last crossed the margin of a *lateral* water hazard two additional options are available[8]:

3. To take a drop within 2 club-lengths of the entry point (point X where the ball last crossed the margin of the lateral water hazard), however not closer to the hole, under PENALTY OF 1 STROKE.
4. To take a drop within 2 club-lengths of the point opposite the entry point (spot on the other side of the lateral water hazard which is at the same distance from the hole), under PENALTY OF 1 STROKE.

Lateral water hazard. *In the case of lateral water hazards (red) the player basically has the same options as with regular water hazards (yellow). In addition, the player can also take a drop on two other spots outside of the water hazard—each of these incurs 1 penalty stroke.*

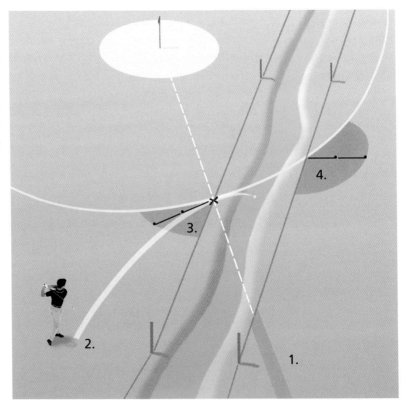

NB: The option of dropping a ball on the so-called line of flight is not provided for by the rules.

Dropping zone. The Committee sometimes specifies a particular area for taking drops and marks it accordingly (the dropping zone). This area is then available to the player as an *additional* option.

Ball in water hazard is playable. It is perfectly possible that a ball comes to rest within the margins of a water hazard with a playable lie. By playing the ball as it lies you can save yourself a penalty stroke. However there are a few points to be taken into consideration (see below).

Playing from a water hazard.
If your ball has a good lie in a water hazard it could definitely make sense to play it. However the ball does actually have to be played just as it lies as relief is practically never given in a water hazard. Furthermore, neither the ground nor the water are to be touched before the stroke is played.

No identification and wrong ball. If you decide to play the ball as it lies you are not permitted to pick it up first in order to identify it[9]. If you cannot tell whether the ball found is your own, but you suspect that this is the case, just play the ball as if it was your own. Then, before playing your first stroke outside the hazard it is imperative that you first check whether it actually was your ball. If you discover that you have been playing with the wrong ball you are to remedy the mistake by returning and playing the correct ball (the wrong ball should be put back). The strokes made with the wrong ball never count and you do NOT INCUR ANY PENALTY STROKES for playing the wrong ball *from a hazard*[10].

Balls close to each other. If two balls happen to land so close together that they obstruct each other, one ball can be marked and picked up until the other one has been played. The ball is then to be put back precisely in its original position. This procedure does NOT INCUR A PENALTY[11].

In a water hazard

Advice and line of play. You are allowed to ask about the pin position, the position of other hazards, out of bounds margins and other matters of public information such as the rules[12]. You are also permitted to inquire about the distance from a fixed object to the green. However you are not allowed to ask about the distance from your ball to the green or questions on how to play a shot as this would be advice[13]. 2 PENALTY STROKES are incurred in the event that advice is asked for or given[14].

If you cannot see the flag from the water hazard you are allowed to ask a fellow-player to indicate the line of play. However the other player must leave this line before you make your stroke[15].

Playing the ball as it lies. If you intend to play your ball from the water hazard you are not permitted to test the condition of the hazard before playing your stroke. You are not allowed to touch the ground nor the water in the hazard. In particular, you are not permitted to ground the club before making a stroke nor to touch the ground or the water on your backswing. A breach of this rule incurs 2 PENALTY STROKES[16].

However you are permitted to touch tall grass when addressing the ball as long as the club is not grounded. You are also allowed to put clubs down in a water hazard.

If you touch the ground or the water as the result of, or to avoid, *falling* this does NOT INCUR A PENALTY in this particular instance[17].

No contact with the ground in a water hazard. Neither the water nor the ground are permitted to be touched in the water hazard before the stroke is played. Therefore the club cannot be grounded, whereas touching high grass is allowed.

Practice swing. In principle, you are also allowed to take practice swings in a water hazard, however in doing so you are not permitted to touch the ground nor the water in the hazard[18]. It might therefore be advisable to make a few practice swings in advance, outside the hazard.

Ball moved when addressing the ball. If your ball moves after you have addressed it (i.e. after taking your stance without grounding your club[19]), it is classed as being moved by you and you must put it back, under PENALTY OF 1 STROKE[20]. If you do not put it back you will incur 2 PENALTY STROKES for playing from the wrong spot[21].

Loose impediments. Loose impediments, such as twigs, leaves, stones etc. must *not* be removed or touched in a water hazard otherwise you will incur 2 PENALTY STROKES[22].

Loose impediments and movable obstructions.
Loose impediments (natural), such as stones, leaves, twigs etc. are not to be removed in a water hazard.
However movable obstructions (artificial), such as the stakes in a water hazard, can be removed, whereby it is important to remember to put them back in exactly the same position after playing your shot.

Obstructions. *Movable* obstructions can be removed from the water hazard WITHOUT PENALTY, as described above (Through the green, see page 98)[23]. If the ground or the water is touched in doing so this is WITHOUT PENALTY[24]. If the ball is moved while doing this it is to be put back WITHOUT PENALTY[25].
On the other hand you are NOT GIVEN FREE RELIEF from *immovable* obstructions, such as bridges, pipes etc. in a water hazard[26]. However if the ball is played as it lies the club is permitted to touch the obstruction (for example the club can be grounded on a bridge).

Abnormal ground conditions. Relief WITHOUT PENALTY IS NOT GIVEN from puddles, GUR and animal tracks in water hazards[27]. The ball has to be played as it lies or it can be dropped in accordance with the water hazard rule (with 1 PENALTY STROKE, see above).

Unplayable lie. You *cannot* declare your ball unplayable in a water hazard[28]. If your ball is in an unplayable position you are allowed to proceed in accordance with the water hazard rule (with 1 PENALTY STROKE, see above) instead of playing it.

Ball hits outside agency/ rub of the green. If your ball hits a stake defining the water hazard or any other "outside agency" this is deemed a rub of the green, you do NOT INCUR A PENALTY and you have to continue playing the ball as it lies[29].

Ball hits the player himself or his equipment. If you yourself or your equipment (golf bag, electric cart etc.) are hit by your ball 2 PENALTY STROKES will be incurred and the ball has to be played as it lies[30].

Ball not hit out of the hazard. If you have played your ball from a water hazard but have not managed to hit it out (e.g. you have hit it further into the hazard) the stroke will of course count but you are still entitled to proceed in accordance with the water hazard rule (with 1 PENALTY STROKE, see above)[31].

Ball hit out of bounds/ lost ball. If you have played your ball from the water hazard and have hit it either out of bounds or to a place where you cannot find it, it is classed as lost in accordance with the rules. You have to drop a new ball on the spot where the last stroke was played from, with 1 PENALTY STROKE—back into the water hazard in this case. However you could also accept ANOTHER 1 STROKE PENALTY (2 PENALTY STROKES in total) and proceed in accordance with the water hazard rule (see above)[32].

Striking the ball more than once. If you strike the ball more than once when playing a shot (e.g. because the club gets caught up in reeds) you have to add 1 PENALTY STROKE to it[33].

No provisional ball. If you hit your ball into a water hazard you do *not* have the option of playing a provisional ball[34]. (This would also be of no benefit at all as the provisional ball is intended to be a means of saving time—in particular to save you walking back. However with a water hazard you have the possibility to take a drop down the course at the spot where the ball entered the hazard, thus dispensing with the need to walk back in most cases.)

Keep it simple. To summarise, we can see that a lot of procedures which are usually allowed are not permitted in a water hazard. However as a player you do not have to remember all these exceptions as in 98% of cases the ball is immersed in the water, i.e. you do not have any choice but to proceed in accordance with the water hazard rule (with 1 PENALTY STROKE, see above).

The many exceptions are only applicable in the rare event that you find your ball in a water hazard and decide to play it as it lies. Even in this case it is virtually impossible to make a mistake if you just bear two points in mind. Do not touch the ground or the water in the hazard before playing your stroke and remember to play the ball exactly as it lies, i.e. do not touch anything and do not try to take relief in any way—removing the stakes is the only measure permitted.

---

1 Note 1 on the definition of "water hazard" and note 1 on the definition of "lateral water hazard".
2 Definition of "water hazard" in conj. with "lateral water hazard".
3 Rule 26-1 in conj. with 27-1. in conj. with 20-5.
4 Rule 13-1. and 4.
5 Rule 26-1.
6 Rule 26-1.b.
7 Rule 26-1.a. in conj. with 20-5.
8 Rule 26-1.c.
9 Rule 12-2.
10 Rule 15-3.
11 Rule 22.
12 Definition of "advice".
13 Decision 8-1/2.
14 Rule 8-1.
15 Rule 8-2.a.
16 Rule 13-4.a. and b.
17 Exception 1. and note on Rule 13-4.
18 Rule 13-4.b.
19 Definition of "addressing the ball".
20 Rule 18-2.b.
21 Rule 20-7.c. in conj. with 18.
22 Rule 13-4.c. and 23.1.
23 Rule 24-1.
24 Exception 1.a. to Rule 13-4.
25 Rule 24-1.
26 Rule 24-2.b.
27 Rule 25-1.b.
28 Rule 28.
29 Rule 19-1.
30 Rule 19-2.b.
31 Rule 26-2.a.
32 Rule 26.2.b.
33 Rule 14-4.
34 Rule 27-2.a.

9. Out of bounds

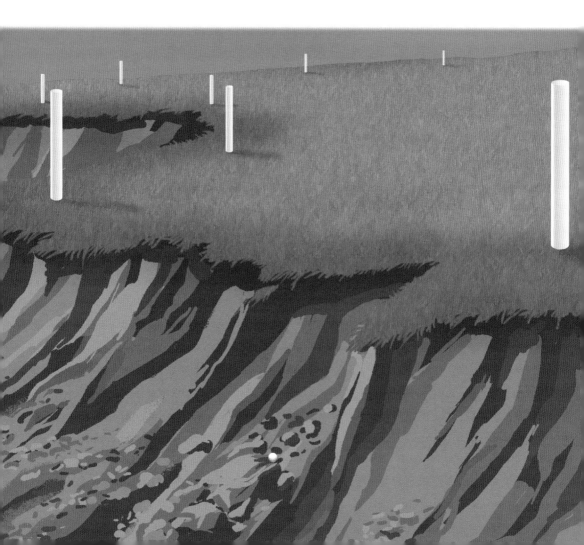

Markings. According to the rules, areas which are out of bounds do not belong to the course. They are usually marked with white posts, lines, fences, walls etc. Sometimes, however, out of bounds is only stipulated in the Local Rules without being marked in white (e.g. "The road which runs along holes … is deemed out of bounds").

Margin. The only factors determining the margin of out of bounds are the markings or if there are posts their connection in a straight line.
A ball is out of bounds when the whole ball lies out of bounds. The markings themselves are out of bounds, i.e. the margin runs on the inside of them.

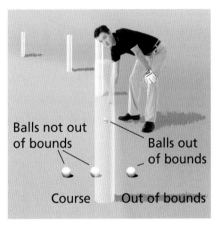

Balls not out of bounds

Balls out of bounds

Course   Out of bounds

Tip. The best way to determine whether a ball is out of bounds is by standing behind a post and bringing it in line with the next post.
Also, watch out for out of bounds margins which are specified in the Local Rules but which may not be marked in white.
Please remember that it makes no sense to spend a long time looking for a ball out of bounds.

Ball out of bounds. A ball which is out of bounds cannot be played any more—it is classed as "lost" in accordance with the rules[2]. You have to bring a new ball into play by returning to the place where you played your last stroke and dropping a ball under PENALTY OF 1 STROKE. If this was on the teeing ground you are permitted to tee-up again[3].
However if you have already played a provisional ball this now becomes the ball in play under PENALTY OF 1 STROKE[4].

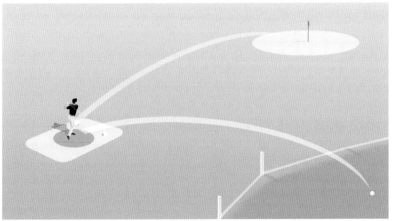

Ball out of bounds. If the ball lands out of bounds the player only has one option—to return to the place where the last stroke was played from and to drop a new ball with a 1 stroke penalty, tee-up on the teeing ground (penalty of stroke and distance).
NB: In particular he does not have the option of dropping a ball where the ball crossed the margin of out of bounds.

Out of bounds

Player out of bounds but ball on the course. A player is permitted to take his stance out of bounds in order to play a ball which is not out of bounds.

In doing so, loose impediments[5] (stones, leaves etc.) and movable obstructions[6] (artificial) which are out of bounds can be removed WITHOUT PENALTY.

However FREE RELIEF IS NOT given from immovable obstructions[7] and abnormal ground conditions[8] (puddles, GUR, animal tracks) in areas which are out of bounds. Removing an out of bounds post would result in 2 PENALTY STROKES[9].

Please note, you are never given free relief from objects which mark out of bounds (posts, fences, nets, walls etc.), whether they are movable or not.

Ball goes out of bounds and comes to rest on the course. If a ball goes out of bounds but then comes to rest on the course (e.g. the ball rebounds from an object out of bounds and flies back onto the course) the ball is not "out" in accordance with the rules. The decisive factor is the spot where the ball comes to rest.

Provisional ball. If your ball has headed out of bounds or towards an area where it may not be possible to find it you would usually play a provisional ball. If you then discover that your original ball actually is out of bounds or if you have not found it within 5 minutes, the provisional ball becomes the ball in play with 1 PENALTY STROKE.

However if you find your original ball and it is still on the course you *have to* continue play with it. You do *not* have the option of continuing to play your provisional ball—even if the original ball has a poor lie and the provisional ball is in a perfect position. Please note that you cannot pronounce the original ball "lost" by declaration. You *have to* pick up the provisional ball as it cannot be played under any circumstances (otherwise you would be DIS-QUALIFIED for playing the wrong ball). The strokes made with the provisional ball do not count.

Even if the original ball is in such a poor lie that it is practically unplayable the provisional ball cannot be declared the ball in play.

If you decide to declare the original ball unplayable you must proceed in strict accordance with the unplayable ball rule (see page 104) and maybe even return to the site of the last stroke once again.

Original ball

Provisional ball

Giving up the provisional ball. If the original ball is found on the course within 5 minutes you have to continue play with it. In this situation the provisional ball cannot become the ball in play under any circumstances.

1 Definition of "out of bounds".	6 Rule 24-1.
2 Definition of "lost ball".	7 Definition of "obstructions".
3 Rule 27-1. in conj. with rule 20-5.	8 Rule 25-1.a.
4 Rule 27-2.b.	9 Rule 13-2.
5 Rule 23-1.	

10. On the green

Green and fringe. The green is the closely-mown area of grass around the hole which is prepared in a special way and is used to putt on. The ball is classed as being on the green when it touches it[1].

As far as the rules are concerned the fringe is not a part of the green but is classed as "through the green" (see page 93ff.), i.e. a ball which is on the fringe is *not* necessarily allowed to be marked, picked up and cleaned[2].

Positioning your equipment. Golf bags and trolleys should be placed off the green in the direction of the next teeing ground. You should also leave your equipment in this position if your ball is in a green bunker or is in the near vicinity of the green, and only take your sand wedge, pitching wedge and putter to the ball. (Then, when you have played your ball onto the green and only need your putter, it is advisable to rest the clubs which you no longer need on the flagstick after it has been removed or on the part of the green which leads to the next tee. This will stop you from leaving your clubs behind—a mistake which often occurs.)

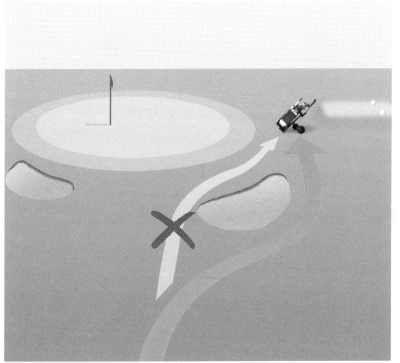

Protecting the green and its near vicinity. *In order to protect the green and its surroundings, neither golf bags nor trolleys are to be placed on the green or on the fringe. The areas between bunkers and the edge of the green also need particular care—please do not pull your golf trolley along this area.*

On the green

Care and maintenance. Please ensure that you do not damage the green with spike marks. You should never run on the green nor should you drag your feet when walking. Stamping your feet in anger or leaping in the air with joy are to be refrained from on the green. You should also take utmost care to ensure that you do not tread on the line of putt of another player, nor on your own line of putt.

Once you have reached the green always start by repairing your ball's pitch mark with a pitch repairer.

If your ball has become embedded in the green you are allowed to mark its position, pick it up and repair the pitch-mark. You can then put the ball back in its original position, WITHOUT PENALTY[3].

(However, if the ball has become embedded in the *fringe* it is to be *dropped*[4] WITHOUT PENALTY as this area is classed as "through the green", see page 103.)

Repairing a pitch mark.
Pitch marks should be repaired as soon as possible. Dig the pitch repairer into the ground at several positions around the pitch mark and draw the grass inwards from the edge of the mark. If you do not have a pitch repairer you can also use a tee if needs be. Finally, it is then advisable to smooth off the grass using the putter. Please also take the time to repair pitch marks which other players have either overlooked or forgotten.

In order to protect the green, no other club except for the putter should ever be used to play on the green.

Marking and putting back the ball. On the green you are permitted to mark the ball's position and then pick it up and clean it[5]. Ideally, the ball should be marked with a ball-marker or a coin.

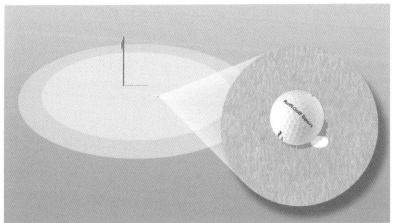

Other players are definitely allowed to mark and pick up your ball (e.g. if your ball is on the line of putt of another player but you are busy in the bunker raking the sand). The rules are fairly relaxed with regards to the person who is to put the ball back—this can either be the person who picked it up or the player himself[6].

Marking a ball to the side. If a ball is on the line of putt of another player it is advisable to move the marker to ensure that it is not possible for the ball to be deflected by it[7]. (If a ball is stopped or deflected by a ball-marker this is classed as a rub of the green—the stroke counts and the ball is to be played as it lies, WITHOUT PENALTY[8].)

It is very important to remember to return the marker to its original position afterwards. If it is not put back and the ball is played from the wrong position the stroke will count and the player will incur 2 PENALTY STROKES for playing from the wrong spot[9].

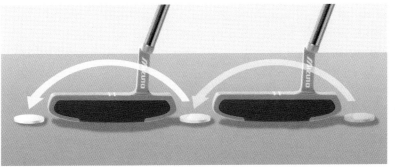

Moving a ball-marker.
It is advisable to move a ball-marker which is interfering with play one or two putter-head lengths to the side. When doing so, aim the putter at a fixed target so that you will be able to move the marker back to exactly the same position afterwards.

Ball or ball-marker moved. If your ball or your ball-marker is moved unintentionally in the process of *marking, lifting or putting back* the ball NO PENALTY is incurred and the ball/ marker must be put back[10].

If, however, the player causes his ball to move when *addressing* it or as a result of a careless *practice swing,* the ball must also be put back—however under PENALTY OF 1 STROKE[11]. If you do not put it back you will incur 2 PENALTY STROKES for playing from the wrong spot[12].

Damaged ball. If your ball has become dented, deformed or significantly damaged in any other way (not just scratched) you are allowed to mark it, pick it up and replace it WITHOUT PEN-

Ball unfit for play.
A damaged ball can be replaced anywhere on the course without penalty. However it is important to inform a fellow-player before doing so.

ALTY. However, before doing so you must inform a fellow-player and give him the opportunity to observe the process. Otherwise you will incur 1 PENALTY STROKE[13].

NB: This procedure is allowed on the entire course, however in practice it is almost only ever used on the green.

Wrong ball. If you realise that the ball you have been playing is not your ball you have to return immediately to the place where you first played the wrong ball from and finish the hole with the correct one. The strokes you have made with the wrong ball do not count[14].

If the first time you played the wrong ball was from a bunker or a water hazard and you have not played any strokes with the wrong ball outside a hazard NO PENALTY STROKES will be incurred. However, if you have played one or more strokes with the wrong ball outside a bunker/ water hazard you will incur 2 PENALTY STROKES[15].

Order of play. On all areas of the golf course it is always the player's turn whose ball is the furthest away from the hole[16]. This general rule also applies on and around the green regardless of whether, for example, one ball is on the green and another is still off it.

However to save time the correct order is often deviated from, especially on the green. If a player is considering playing out of turn he should always discuss this with his fellow-competitors in advance. Not keeping to the correct order of play does NOT INCUR A PENALTY as long as no agreement has been made with the intention of giving one of the players a tactical advantage (e.g. in order to enable a player to see how the green is going to break)—in this case they would be punished with DISQUALIFICATION[17].

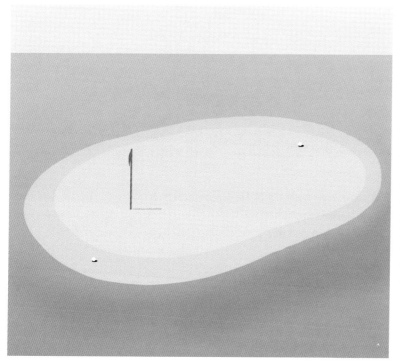

Different order. In the example shown, the ball on the right is on the green whilst the ball on the left is on the fringe, i.e. off the green. Strictly speaking, the ball on the right would have to be played first as it is furthest away from the hole. The flag would have to be removed from the hole to do this. Then, if requested by the player on the left, the flag would have to be put back in and subsequently removed once again. Therefore to save time the official order is often deviated from in such cases until all the balls are on the green.

Even if it is not your turn to play you should still prepare for your shot by reading the line of putt. However in doing so you should make sure that you do not disturb any other players.

Advice and line of putt. Information given on the speed of the green, its break and on the line of putt etc. would be advice[18]. Therefore the only people you are permitted to ask about these matters are your *caddie* or *team partner*, should you have one[19]. If your caddie or team partner indicates the line of putt he is allowed to point to a spot on the green but, in doing so, he is not permitted to touch the green—if he did the player would be given 2 PENALTY STROKES[20].

On the green

Where to stand. *No one is permitted to stand on the backwards extension of the line of putt while a player is playing his shot. Also, no one should stand behind the hole on the extension of the line of putt as players usually find this distracting.*

Playing the ball as it lies. Generally speaking, the line of putt should not be touched and it should definitely not be improved[21]. An exception to this is repairing pitch marks and old hole plugs (places where the hole used to be)[22]. If you would like to repair areas such as these which are on the line of putt it is advisable to inform a fellow-player in advance in order to avoid any misunderstandings. Spike marks on the line of putt are annoying but unfortunately they cannot be repaired[23]. Out of courtesy they should be smoothed out using the putter *after* the hole has been completed so that subsequent players are presented with a flawless green.

You are not allowed to test the surface of the putting green by rolling a ball or by roughening the surface of the green or scraping it[24]. However you are entitled to read the green i.e. to use your eyes only to examine and assess the green with respect to turf conditions and gradients, in order to determine the ideal line of putt.

Careless putting. The ball is always to be hit, not pushed or scraped—otherwise 2 PENALTY STROKES are incurred. However you are allowed to hit it with any side of the putter head e.g. even with the back of the putter[25].

Putting. *When putting, the ball is always to be hit with the head of the club—the club is not to be used like a billiard cue. Having said this, you are permitted to use any side of the club head you like e.g. the tip or the back of the club are also allowed.*

However you are not permitted to stand astride the line of putt or its backwards extension (like when playing croquet).

Loose impediments. Loose impediments, such as stones, leaves, twigs etc. can be removed from the green WITHOUT PENALTY[26]. On the green, loose soil and sand are also classed as loose impediments[27]. You are allowed to pick them up individually or carefully brush them to the side—as long as you do not smooth out uneven areas on the line of putt in doing so[28].

If the ball moves when a loose impediment is being removed this does NOT INCUR A PENALTY (this exception applies to the green only) and the ball must be put back as always[29] (however it is more prudent to mark the ball and pick it up before removing an impediment so that the ball will not be moved in the first place).

Loose impediments.
Sand and loose soil are only classed as loose impediments on the green. Therefore sand which has sprayed over the edge of the bunker can only be removed without penalty on the green. It must be left where it is on the fringe and in all other areas.

Obstructions. *Movable* obstructions, such as lost gloves, score cards, pencils and other artificial objects can be removed from the green WITHOUT PENALTY, as is also the case everywhere else on the course. If the ball moves as a result—put it back, WITHOUT PENALTY[30].

You are also given relief from *immovable* obstructions on the green—however they are practically never found on the green (in rare instances sprinklers might be installed into very large greens). You are given FREE RELIEF from them if they interfere with your stance, swing or line of putt[31]. The procedure for relief is the same as for abnormal ground conditions on the green[32] (see below).

However please bear in mind that you are NEVER GIVEN FREE RELIEF from immovable obstructions which are simply on your *line of play* (in contrast to the line of putt, this term is used if the ball is not yet on the green)[33].

Sprinkler heads. Sprinklers are usually installed off the green, on the fringe. As the rules designate this area "through the green" the player is only given relief if the sprinkler interferes with his stance or swing. If, as shown in the illustration, the sprinkler is only on the line of play the ball has to be played as it lies. (However if the ball was on the green and a sprinkler was on the line of putt the player would be entitled to free relief.)

Abnormal ground conditions. You are also given FREE RELIEF from abnormal ground conditions (puddles, ground under repair, animal tracks) on the green. This not only applies to cases when the stance or the swing is interfered with but also if these conditions are on the line of putt[34]. In this case the nearest point is to be determined (not necessarily on the green but definitely not in a hazard) which eliminates the interference to the largest possible extent and the ball is to be *placed* on this spot (in this position exactly and not within 1 club-length which would be the case with a puddle through the green or in a bunker)[35].

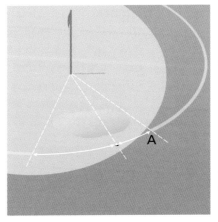

Puddle on the green.
Point A is the nearest point of relief, therefore the ball can be placed there without penalty even though it is no longer on the green.
If the ball was still off the green it would have to be played as it lies as in this case the puddle would only be on the line of play and not on the line of putt.

Tending the flag. The player whose ball is the nearest to the hole is usually the one who tends the flag.

When tending the flag you should ensure that your shadow does not fall on the hole or on the player's line of putt. If necessary, hold onto the flag on the flagstick so that it does not flutter in the wind and disturb the concentration of the player who is about to take his putt. Always stand at the side of the hole and not behind it.

Loosen the flagstick before the player takes his putt as it could be stuck. Pull the flagstick out of the hole immediately and without hesitation after the player has taken his putt. Please ensure that the rim of the hole is not damaged when removing the flagstick. When no more players require the flag to be tended put it down carefully, off the green if possible.

Tending the flag. *When tending the flagstick it is advisable to stand at the side and hold the flag still. Furthermore, please ensure that your shadow does not fall on the hole or on the line of putt.*

Ball hits flagstick. When you are taking a putt on the green the ball is not allowed to hit the flagstick otherwise you will incur 2 PENALTY STROKES[36]. Therefore you should ask someone to tend the flag or have it removed from the hole and make sure that it is put down in a place where you are not likely to hit it.

If you have played a ball from off the green or have even holed-out directly, hitting the flagstick comes WITHOUT PENALTY (you only incur 2 PENALTY STROKES when you take a putt *on the green* and hit the flagstick)[37].

Ball wedged on the flag-stick. This ball is not classed as holed because it is not yet below the edge of the hole. However this is no cause for concern as holing-out in this case is only a formality— carefully pull the flagstick out so that the ball falls into the hole and is classed as holed without an additional stroke.

If your ball only falls halfway into the hole, i.e. if it is stuck between the flagstick and the edge of the hole, you are permitted to remove the flagstick carefully so that the ball falls all the way into the hole. It is then deemed to have been holed with the last stroke[38].

Ball hits another ball. When you take a putt on the green your ball is not allowed to hit any other balls on the green, otherwise you will incur 2 PENALTY STROKES[39]. Therefore you should ask other players to mark and pick up their balls if there is a chance that they might interfere with your game. (If you hit a ball on the green after having played from *off* the green NO PENALTY is incurred[40].)

Ball hits another ball. If, when putting on the green, you hit another player's ball you will be given 2 penalty strokes. You then have to play your ball as it lies—the ball which was hit must be put back.

Ball close to the hole. If a ball comes to rest just in front of the hole and there is only a short distance left to the hole, the order of play is usually disregarded so that the player can "tap it in". However a player who is considering playing in the wrong order should ask the other players in advance to make sure that this is okay.

If a ball comes to rest directly on the edge of the hole you are allowed to wait for 10 seconds. If the ball falls into the hole within these 10 seconds it is deemed to have been holed with the last stroke[41].

The 10 second rule.
If your ball comes to rest on the edge of the hole you are allowed to wait 10 seconds. If the ball falls into the hole within this time it is classed as having been holed. If it falls in after 10 seconds it is also classed as holed but you have to add another stroke to your score.

Holing the ball. The ball has been holed when it comes to *rest below* the rim of the hole[42]. If a ball falls into the hole and then springs back out again it must be hit back into the hole.

If, when holing-out, you hit another ball which is already in the hole, this does NOT INCUR A PENALTY[43]. However it is established practice to take your ball out of the hole immediately after holing it. Always take the ball out of the hole using your hand and never try to shovel it out with the head of your putter as this could damage the rim of the hole. Make sure you do not lean on your putter when taking the ball out of the hole.

No conceding. Strokes *cannot* be conceded in a stroke play competition. If a player picks up his ball by mistake he has to put it back with 1 PENALTY STROKE and then hole it[44]. If he does not he will be DISQUALIFIED[45].

Replacing the flagstick. The player who holed-out first is usually the person to replace the flagstick when the hole has been completed. Please ensure that you do not damage the edge of the hole in doing so.

It would be most impolite to just leave the green after holing-out if your fellow-players have not yet finished the hole. You should therefore wait by the green until everyone else has holed-out and then all go together to the next tee.

On the green

Announcing your score. After completing a hole you should inform your fellow-players, especially your marker, of the number of strokes you have taken. However only do this after all the players have completed the hole and not straight after holing-out. Otherwise, if you and your fellow-competitors have counted a different number of strokes, this might disturb the concentration of those players still waiting to take their putts.

Freeing up the green. Please leave the green immediately after completing it and only record your number of strokes at the next tee. To keep up the pace of the game the player who has the honour should tee-off straight away and only fill in the score card afterwards.

Practice putts. When you have finished the hole, you are allowed to putt again for practice if this does not delay play. *Putting and chipping* on the green of the hole just played or at the next teeing ground is permitted *between* holes[46].

Double green. If your ball lands on a double green in the area of the wrong hole you have to play the ball as it lies. If the wrong hole is in your way you are entitled to relief as this hole is classed as ground under repair. Place the ball at the nearest point where the hole is no longer in the way, WITHOUT PENALTY[47] (also see page 142f.).

Wrong green. If your ball lands on the wrong green you are not allowed to play the ball. You *have to* take FREE RELIEF[48] (see page 103).

146

1 Definition of "green".
2 Rule 18-2.a. in conj. with definition of "through the green".
3 Rule 16-1.b. and c.
4 Rule 25-2.
5 Rule 16-1.b.
6 Rule 20-3.a.
7 Note on Rule 20-1.
8 Rule 19-1.
9 Rule 20-7.c. in conj. with Rule 18.
10 Rule 18-2.a. in conj. with Rule 20-1. and 3.a.
11 Rule 18-2.a. and b.
12 Rule 20-7.c. in conj. with Rule 18.
13 Rule 5-3.
14 Rule 15-3.b.
15 Ibid.
16 Rule 10-2.b.
17 Rule 10-2.c.
18 Definition of "advice".
19 Rule 8-1.
20 Rule 8-2.b.
21 Rule 16-1.a.
22 Rule 16-1.c.
23 Ibid.
24 Rule 16-1.d.

25 Rule 14-1.
26 Rule 23-1.
27 Definition of "loose impediments".
28 Rule 16-1.a.(i).
29 Rule 18-2.a. in conj. with Rule 23-1.
30 Rule 24-1.
31 Rule 24-2.a.
32 Rule 24-2.b.(iii).
33 Rule 24-2.a.
34 Rule 25-1.a.
35 Rule 25-1.b.(iii)
36 Rule 17-3.
37 Rule 17-3.c.
38 Rule 17-4.
39 Rule 19-5.a.
40 Ibid.
41 Rule 16-2.
42 Definition of "holed".
43 Rule 19-5.a. in conj. with definition of "ball in play".
44 Rule 18-2.a.
45 Rule 3-2.
46 Rule 7-2.
47 Definition of "ground under repair" in conj. with Rule 25-1.a. and b.
48 Rule 25-3.

11. After the round

Thanking for the game. It is customary to shake hands after finishing the last hole, to thank each other for the game and to congratulate players if appropriate.

__Thanks for the round.__
Shaking hands after the round is a friendly gesture. Headwear should be removed before doing so as a matter of courtesy.

Checking and completing the score card. Compare the number of strokes for each hole recorded by your marker with those you noted down yourself to make sure they are the same. Do this by reading them out to each other or by holding the two score cards next to each other.

Avoid making any errors, unclear entries and jottings on the score card. An incorrect entry should not simply be written over—it is better to cross it out and record the correct score next to it. It is advisable for the marker to confirm the new entry with his signature.

If, during the round, you encountered a situation where you were uncertain about the rules and therefore decided to play two balls, you must now clarify the matter with the Committee. You are to inform the Committee of the incident in every case so that they can decide which of the scores should stand—even if you made the same score with both of the balls[1].

The score card must then be signed by both the marker and the player[2].

Carefully check all the entries one more time (name, handicap, number of strokes, signatures of the player and the marker) and check that your score is recorded in the *player* column. Then cross out the scores in the marker column so as to minimise the risk of any misunderstandings.

Comparing score cards.
The score card is an important document. Check it carefully and make sure that it has been signed by the marker and the player before handing it in.

Returning the score card. Hand the score card in to the pro shop or the secretary's office (or to any other place designated by the Committee) without delay[3]. The score card must be handed in after every competition—even if the player is not happy with his result. Not handing in a score card would be extremely unsportsmanlike and this type of conduct would usually result in disciplinary measures.

Calculation. It is not necessary for you to add up the results and calculate the number of points—this is carried out by the Committee. If, despite this, the player decides to count up his strokes/ points and makes a mistake in doing so, he will not be penalised in any way. The player is only responsible for ensuring that his strokes are recorded correctly for each hole[4].

After the round

Returning an incorrect score card. A score card cannot be corrected once it has been handed in[1]. If you have entered too many strokes for a hole this number will stand[5]. If you have handed in a score card with too few strokes for a hole, or if it has not been signed, you will be DISQUALIFIED[6].

Shoes. Please do not forget to clean your shoes thoroughly before entering the clubhouse. Bear in mind that in some areas of the clubhouse wearing golf shoes, especially those with spikes, could be forbidden.

Having a drink. After the round it is customary to have a drink together with your fellow-players in the clubhouse (the club bar is therefore laughingly referred to as the 19th hole).

Never-ending stories. If someone asks you how the game went it is advisable only to answer with your result (number of strokes/ number of Stableford points). It is better not to relate the story of your entire golf round and what would have happened if…— experience has shown that absolutely no one is interested.

Prize giving. It is a sign of a sportsmanlike attitude and respect to wait until the prize giving ceremony even if you are not amongst the winners yourself. If you are not going to take part in the ceremony you should send your apologies.

---

1 Rule 3-3.a.
2 Rule 6-6.a. and b.
3 Rule 6-6.b.
4 Rule 6-6.d. and decision 6-6d/2.

5 Rule 6-6.c.
6 Rule 6-6.d.
7 Rule 6-6.b. and d.

IV. Summary

Etiquette

- Always ensure that no one will be put at risk due to a swing or stroke which you are about to make.

- If someone could be endangered by your ball, even if the probability of being hit is only slight, then call fore immediately several times and as loudly as possible.

- If you yourself hear someone shout fore duck down immediately and protect your head with your arms.

- Always play and walk at a good pace and avoid unnecessary loss of time.

- Slower players are to let following players pass. The following group is to be invited to play through by means of a clear signal.

- Please care for and maintain the course whenever possible.

- Please conduct yourself in a quiet, fair manner on the course and avoid any sort of conduct which could disturb other players.

- Ensure that your equipment is in compliance with the rules and etiquette, and is complete.

- A plea to the men—keep your impatience in check especially if you play golf together with ladies.

In short:
Always conduct yourself in the way that you would like others to conduct themselves.

Summary

	Through the green	In the bunker	In a water hazard	On the green
Marking the ball and picking it up to identify it.	Permitted without penalty.	✗	✗	Permitted without penalty.
Addressing the ball.	Taking the stance and placing the club on the ground.	Taking the stance (do not place the club on the ground).	Taking the stance (do not place the club on the ground).	Taking the stance and placing the club on the ground.
Ball moved after being addressed.	The ball has to be put back under penalty of 1 stroke.			
Loose impediments (leaves, twigs, stones etc.).	Remove without penalty.	✗	✗	Remove without penalty.
Ball moved when loose impediment has been removed.	Put the ball back, 1 penalty stroke.	—	—	Put the ball back without penalty.
Movable obstructions (drink cans, bench, rake etc.).	Remove without penalty (if the ball is lying in or on the movable obstruction—mark the position of the ball, remove the obstruction without penalty and then drop the ball as near as possible to the spot marked. If this spot is on the green the ball is to be placed).			
Ball moved when movable obstruction has been removed.	The ball has to be put back without penalty.			

Immovable obstructions (road, house, wall etc.). Relief is given when the obstruction interferes with the ball's lie, stance or swing (an obstruction on the line of play alone is not sufficient).	Determine the nearest point where you can take your stance and swing without interference from the *obstruction* and drop the ball within 1 club-length, without penalty.	Very rare case. (The player has two options to take a drop: 1. *Without penalty in the bunker* within 1 club-length of the nearest point of relief. 2. *With 1 penalty stroke outside of the* bunker, on the backwards extension of the line from the hole to the ball.)	✗	Practically unimaginable. (Relief is given also if line of putt is interfered with: Determine the nearest point where you can take your stance and swing and putt without interference from the obstruction. Place the ball in this spot exactly, without penalty.)
Abnormal ground conditions (puddle, GUR, animal tracks). Relief is given when the ball's lie, stance or swing is interfered with (interference of the line of play alone is not sufficient).	Determine the nearest point where you can take your stance and swing without interference from the *abnormal ground conditions* and drop the ball within 1 club-length, without penalty.	The player has two options to take a drop: 1. *Without penalty in the bunker* within 1 club-length of the nearest point where the interference is eliminated to the *largest possible* extent. 2. *With 1 penalty stroke outside of the* bunker, on the backwards extension of the line from the hole to the ball.	✗	Relief is also given if the line of putt is interfered with: Determine the nearest point where you can take your stance and swing and putt without interference from these conditions to the *largest possible* extent. Place the ball in this spot exactly (even if this is off the green), without penalty.

Summary

	Through the green	In the bunker	In a water hazard	On the green
Ball lost in abnormal ground conditions.	Relief without penalty as described above, however the starting point is now the point where the ball last crossed the margin of the abnormal ground conditions.	Relief without penalty as described above, however the starting point is now the point where the ball last crossed the margin of the abnormal ground conditions.	✗	Practically unimaginable. (Relief without penalty as described above, however the starting point is the point where the ball entered the abnormal ground conditions.)
Relief for a ball which is embedded in its own pitch mark.	Only on *closely-mown* areas (fairway, fringe), pick the ball up, clean it and drop it as near as possible to the original position, without penalty.	✗	✗	Mark the ball, pick it up and clean it. Repair the pitch mark and then put the ball back without penalty.
Unplayable ball.	Under penalty of 1 stroke drop a ball 1. within 2 club-lengths. 2. on the backwards extension of the line from the hole to the ball. 3. on the site of the last stroke.	Under penalty of 1 stroke drop a ball 1. within 2 club-lengths *in the bunker.* 2. on the backwards extension of the line from the hole to the ball *in the bunker.* 3. on the site of the last stroke.	✗ (Proceed in accordance with the water hazard rule.)	Practically unimaginable. (3 options to *drop* a ball as described under "through the green".)

154

Playing the wrong ball.	The strokes with the wrong ball do not count—the player incurs 2 penalty strokes and has to return and play the correct ball.	The strokes with the wrong ball do not count—the mistake remains *without penalty* and the player has to return and play the correct ball.	The strokes with the wrong ball do not count—the mistake remains *without penalty* and the player has to return and play the correct ball.	The strokes with the wrong ball do not count—the player incurs 2 penalty strokes and has to return and play the correct ball.
Lost ball.	Drop a new ball at the place where the last stroke was played from under penalty of 1 stroke (tee-up on the teeing ground).	Drop a new ball at the place where the last stroke was played from under penalty of 1 stroke (tee-up on the teeing ground).	Drop a new ball at the place where the last stroke was played from under penalty of 1 stroke (tee-up on the teeing ground) or proceed in accordance with the water hazard rule.	Practically unimaginable.
Playing a provisional ball.	Permitted without penalty*. (*A penalty stroke has to be added only once the provisional ball becomes the ball in play.)	Permitted without penalty*.	If the ball lands in a water hazard a provisional ball *cannot* be played. Proceed in accordance with the water hazard rule	Practically unimaginable

V. Match play rules

Principle. In principle, the same rules apply to match play as they do to stroke play. However, whereas during stroke play the basic penalty for a breach of the rules is 2 penalty strokes, in match play the player immediately loses the hole[1].

However the following special factors must be taken into account in match play.

Winner. In match play, opponents play against each other on a hole by hole basis. The winner of the hole is the player who holes-out with the fewest number of strokes (in a handicap match the lowest net result for the hole is decisive)[2]. A hole is halved when both players achieve the same result[3]. The winner of the entire match is the player who won the most holes on the round. Therefore a match play round comes to an end as soon as a player leads by more holes than there are left to play[4].

Concessions. In match play the ball does not necessarily have to be holed-out. A player can concede that his opponent has holed out with his next stroke—even if the ball is still a considerable distance from the hole. He can even concede a hole or the entire match at any time before it is completed[5].
NB: If a player's next shot is conceded, e.g. a short putt, but he decides to play the stroke anyway it is still classed as having been conceded even if he misses the shot—once conceded, always conceded; conceded shots can neither be refused nor withdrawn[6]. (Holing out after the shot or the hole has been conceded is not considered unauthorised practicing, as you are always allowed to finish playing a hole for which the result has already been settled[7].)

Practicing on the course. On the day of a match play competition the player is permitted to practice on the competition course before the round[8].

Honour. The person who won the previous hole has the honour at the tee[9].

Playing from outside the teeing ground. If a player tees-off from outside the teeing ground this comes WITHOUT PENALTY in match play, however the opponent can immediately require the player to cancel his stroke and replay it by teeing-off from within the teeing ground[10].

Playing out of turn. If a player plays in the wrong order this usually comes WITHOUT PENALTY in match play as well. However the opponent is permitted to require the player to cancel this stroke and repeat it in the correct order. A ball is then to be played from the spot which is as close as possible to the position where the last stroke was played from (drop the ball, tee it up on the teeing ground, place it on the green)[11].

Information on the number of strokes. In match play every player has the right to receive information on the current score and the number of strokes taken by his opponent. If a player has incurred a penalty while playing a hole he must inform his opponent of this as soon as possible. If he does not do so it is classed as providing incorrect information, even if he himself is not aware that he has incurred a penalty. Providing incorrect information is usually punished with the LOSS OF THE HOLE[12].

Ball at rest moved by opponent. If the player's *ball at rest* is moved by an opponent, *except for during a search,* the opponent incurs 1 PENALTY STROKE, and the ball must be put back[13]. If, however, the player's ball is moved by an opponent while at rest and *while it is being looked for,* he does NOT INCUR A PENALTY and the ball must be put back in this case as well[14].

Ball in motion deflected or stopped by the opponent. If the *moving* ball hits the opponent or his equipment and is therefore unintentionally deflected or stopped this is classed as a rub of the green in match play as well and NO PENALTY is incurred. However in match play, the player is then permitted to choose whether he wants to continue to play the ball as it lies or to immediately cancel the stroke and replay it by dropping a ball WITHOUT PENALTY as near as possible to the position where the last stroke was played from (teeing up on the teeing ground, placing it on the green)[15].

Match play rules

Player and opponent mistake each others' balls for their own. If the *player and the opponent* mistake their ball for each others', the player who *first* played the wrong ball outside a hazard is the one to LOSE THE HOLE. If this cannot be determined the hole must be played to the end with the exchanged balls[16].

Ball hits another ball on the green. If, when putting on the green, a player's ball hits another ball at rest this does NOT INCUR A PENALTY in match play[17] (however the ball moved does, of course, still have to be put back[18]).

If in doubt about the rules. In match play you do *not* have the option to play a second ball if you are unsure about the rules[19]. The players must find a solution themselves and continue the game without delay. If a player does not agree with the course of action taken by his opponent, he can make an objection and clarify the point with the Committee after the round. However a prerequisite for this is that he makes a formal "claim" immediately, and explicitly informs his opponent of this, stating his reasons[20].

---

1 Rule 2-6.
2 Rule 2-1.
3 Rule 2-2.
4 Rule 2-3.
5 Rule 2-4.
6 Decision 2-4/6.
7 Rule 7-2.
8 Rule 7-1.a.
9 Rule 10-1.a.
10 Rule 11-4.a.

11 Rule 10-1.c. in conj. with rule 20-5.
12 Rule 9-2.
13 Rule 18-3.b.
14 Rule 18-3.a.
15 Rule 19-3. in conj. with rule 20-5.
16 Rule 15-3.a.
17 Rule 19-5.a.
18 Ibid.
19 Rule 3-3.a.
20 Rule 2-5.

VII. Index

Index

Index

Use the rules to your advantage!

As this book is too large to carry around in your golf bag, we have produced a compact version, containing the most important rules—*"Golf Rules Quick Reference Stroke Play Guide"*, a handy, waterproof, ring-bound book which provides fast, easy-to-understand answers to all the frequently occurring rules questions.

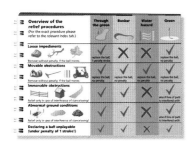

Step 1
The overview shows whether you are entitled to relief.

Step 2
If you are, find the index tab which corresponds to the position of your ball.

Step 3
Use the headings to find the right solution for your particular situation.

Awarded the sensational second prize in the search for the best new products of the year 2004!

(PGA Merchandise Show in Orlando/Florida—the world's largest golf exhibition.)

Golf Rules Quick Reference Stroke Play Guide
Your handy rules guide for use on the golf course
by Yves Ton-That, 40 pages, colour, illustrated, plastic coated and spiral-bound.
Artigo Publishing International, 1ˢᵗ edition 2004, ISBN 3-909596-02-9

Available in book shops, in pro shops
or under www.golfrulesmadeeasy.com

Golf rules can be entertaining

What do you do if a goat eats your ball?

What happens if the ball lands in a cowpat and why should married couples not play Greensomes?

Who cheated where, when and why?

You'll find the answers to these and other crucial questions in Yves Ton-That's latest book. The most important rules, which are normally rather difficult to digest, are explored in bite-sized pieces with the aid of 14 hilarious stories. An extremely informative and enjoyable read—even those who are not particularly interested in the rules will find this book tremendously entertaining. The book's superb illustrations make it especially suitable as a gift.

"Finally a book that gets the rules across in an entertaining way. The most important rules are explained in 14 amusing stories. Golf rules really can be fun!"

Golf-Time

Coming soon

Should I Take a Drop or What...?
A collection of hilarious stories about the rules of golf
by Yves Ton-That, 171 pages, illustrated, hardcover.
Artigo Publishing International

Available in book shops, in pro shops
or under www.golfrulesmadeeasy.com